Y0-CJG-483

THE CRAB BOOK

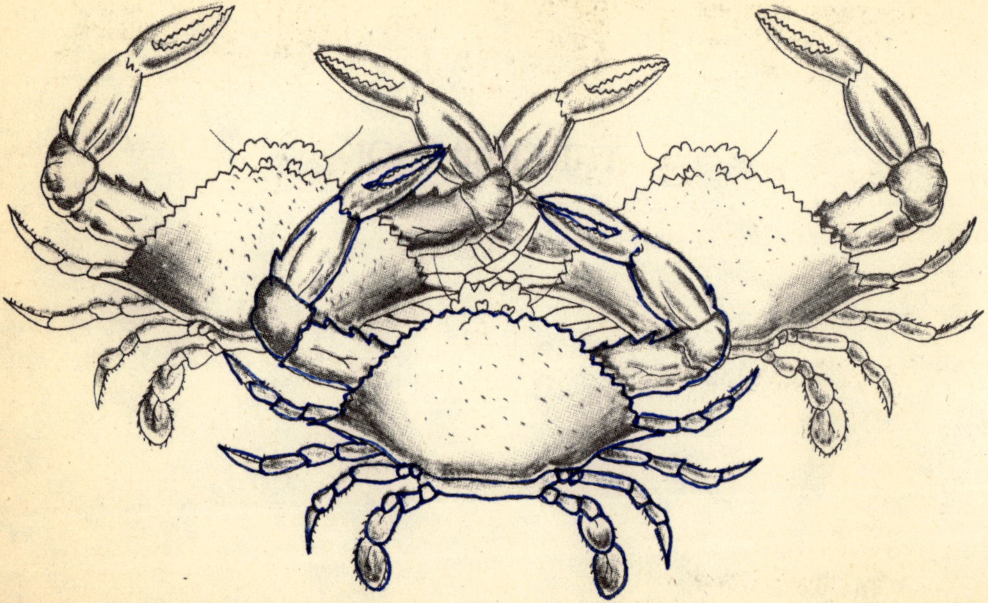

THE CRAB BOOK

How to Catch, Cook and Eat Crabs

Cy and Pat Liberman

The Middle Atlantic Press
Wilmington, Delaware

THE CRAB BOOK

A MIDDLE ATLANTIC PRESS BOOK

TX
754
.C83
L52
1985

Copyright © 1978 by Cy and Pat Liberman
All rights reserved. No part of this publication may be reproduced or transmitted in any form or by any means, electronic or mechanical, including photocopy, recording, or any information storage and retrieval system, without permission in writing from the publisher.

First Middle Atlantic Printing, June 1985
Second printing 1987

Text illustrations by Rosa Goldfind
Text design by Joyce C. Weston

ISBN: 0-912608-22-6

The Middle Atlantic Press, Inc.
848 Church Street
Wilmington, DE 19899

CONTENTS

1. About Crabs — 1
2. How to Catch Crabs — 14
3. How to Steam and Eat Crabs — 55
4. Cooking with Crabs — 82
A Note on Nutrition — 152

To the Crab

*Inside the amazing crab
Is an alchemist's kind of lab.
It will take what the sea has discarded—
Old fish, never highly regarded,
Sundry sea creatures, living and dead,
Like the tail of an eel, or its head,
And convert it (a fabulous feat)
Into crab—the world's greatest meat.*

*Ah, the succulent white meat he makes!
Those delicious, ambrosial flakes!
Well, that's why we urge admiration
For this most delightful crustacean.*

ABOUT CRABS

People speak of the seven wonders of the world. Without evaluating the seven, we claim the eighth is crabs. Surely, crabs are one of Mother Nature's most amazing creations. They take various cast-off vegetable and animal matter and convert it into the world's most delicious meat for humans. Without delving at all into the crab's secrets about how he (and she) makes this miraculous conversion, we are content to admire the results. We praise the crab. We enjoy catching him and her without discrimination. We delight in consuming the meat of the cooked crab in a great many different ways. Some are even better than others. We have never made a crab dish we did not like. But others can manage it.

If we were put on diets that limited us to one kind of meat there is no doubt whatsoever that we would choose crab as that meat. Actually, we've never had that limitation imposed. But when crabs are plentiful where we live on Chesapeake Bay, and we can easily catch all we can eat, we eat very little of any other meat. We happily consume different crab dishes for dinner every night and often have others for lunch. We'll do it with supreme pleasure anytime the crabs cooperate while we're still agile enough to scoop them up in a net, or pull up our crab pot and get the kicking crabs to the steaming water.

What we want to do in this volume is to share with you our enthusiasm for getting, cooking and eating crabs by explaining in detail how to do those three pleasurable things. We won't get technical about it. If you're interested in more than we're going to report on the life cycle of the crab, or its anatomy and sex habits (which do not set a good example for humans), you can readily find out about those subjects in other publications. We're not greatly interested in the sex life of the crab. We're interested in having crabs know all about that and reproducing in suitable volume so that all of us can be interested in the adult crab as delectable food for discriminating humans.

Those of us who are fortunate enough to live near Chesapeake Bay are in the greatest crab producing area in the world. But let's skip the figures. Let's get on with how to get a share of the marvelous blue crabs of the bay, and their close relatives up and down the Atlantic Coast. We're hooked on the Atlantic blue crab which makes its home in the bay and nearby waters, and also inhabits many other bays and rivers along the coast. We'll admit that many other varieties of crabs are excellent to eat, but the Atlantic blue crab comes first with us.

So, let's see how to get them, and then look into the cooking and eating of the blue beauties.

1. BUYING CRABS

There are two ways to get good crabs for your dining pleasure at home. One is to buy them; the other is to catch them, which is more fun. If you're short on time or energy, or not in the right place to lure the blue crabs from the water yourself, or you're hungry for them out of season, select a reliable seafood market and see if live crabs or fresh crab meat are available. If not, you can buy canned crab meat, if you insist. We try to avoid it. It's expensive and, we think, less flavorful than the others. But it's convenient to get, easy to keep, and available in all seasons.

　　Seafood markets and seafood counters of big food stores sometimes have blue crabs in three forms—hard shell crabs, soft shell crabs and fresh crab meat. They generally have the fresh crab meat all year; some have live or steamed hard shell crabs in summer. But only the specialized seafood markets, or stores at or near the waterfront, are likely to have live soft shell crabs. However, seafood dealers serving restaurants have frozen soft shell crabs available all year.

If you're starting out in pursuit of the pleasure of crab eating, your first step should be to go to a restaurant that serves steamed hard shell crabs and order some, preferably with a friend who knows how to go about eating them. Yes, there are very detailed instructions in this book, if you don't have a friend to show you the technique. Or, as an alternate first step into the world of crab feasting, you could buy a can of fresh crab meat and make any of the cold or hot dishes we recommend in later chapters.

When you're ready to buy live hard shell crabs for use at home, there are a few things to know. First, buy only those that are still definitely and visibly alive. Accept no dead ones even if the vendor alleges they were alive "a few minutes ago." You want them alive not only at the store, but until you put them in the pot to be steamed. Second, the price depends on the size of the crabs. Usually the bigger crab at the higher price is the better buy. Big ones are much easier to work with—you waste a lot in handling the smaller fellows.

You don't have to worry about the designations of sizes. If the biggest ones available are called "number ones," they're the crabs you want in most cases. What really counts in crabs is the amount of white meat inside. There are times when the medium-sized crabs are running relatively heavier than the larger ones—that is, the smaller crab is more solidly filled with meat and the larger one hasn't yet filled up his new shell. Ask the dealer if one size is running "heavier" than another. Later, when you get some experience, you can feel the difference. It would make sense to sell crabs by weight rather than by dozens, but that's not how it's done.

Now, what about those roadside trucks with CRABS in big letters? Okay for live hard shell crabs if every crab is alive and moving. The same is true for crummy looking little stores in poor neighborhoods of cities even if they sell nothing but crabs. We don't buy steamed crabs from any of those loosely rooted specialists. We buy steamed crabs only from a source we can trust absolutely to have started the steaming process with every crab alive and complaining. That means a reliable, established seafood dealer or restaurant.

It's really more satisfactory to buy the live crabs and steam them yourself. However, if you want the job done for you, find a place that will not insist on putting a lot of seasoning "salt" on the crabs when they are put in a basket or bag for you. Unless you've tried them that way, and know you like it, get the crabs without that hot seasoning. It's what the restaurants use to make you thirsty so that you'll buy a lot of beer with your crabs. Who needs it? We prefer the crabs without any of it. We wash the stuff off if we forget to order them without it. Try crabs both ways some time; see what you like.

Next, about buying fresh crab meat. The first thing that may shock you is the price. But after you have picked a few dozen crabs yourself to get the meat to make those wonderful crab entrees, you'll appreciate the labor it requires. We don't feel badly about paying the price for fresh crab meat when we have a desire for it and can't catch crabs.

When you're satisfied about the price and ready to buy fresh crab meat, buy it only where it is in a refrigerator and is not only cold, but is actually sitting on, and preferably surrounded by, crushed ice. That's the way it keeps best. Crab meat is difficult to keep for long; it's best to buy it where there's a steady turnover. That's why we try to get it at a seafood market rather than a seafood counter.

Fresh crab meat, picked by hand, comes in an unsealed can, often with a transparent plastic lid so that you can admire the white contents. The white may be speckled with yellow flecks of fat. You can also buy hand or machine picked crab meat that has been pasteurized and put in a sealed can, like tomatoes. If you buy the unpasteurized, hand picked, fresh crab meat—which we prefer—make sure it is cold when you get it. Then, when you get home, immediately put the can in a bowl, surround the can with cracked ice, and put the can and bowl combination in your refrigerator until you're ready to make a crab dish. The alternative, of course, is to delay buying the crab meat until you're ready to use it. If the weather is warm and the trip home is a long one, get the crab meat in an insulated bag with ice, or take along a small icebox.

Machine picked crab meat is a new wrinkle. Several inventors have recently developed complex gadgets that manage to extract the delicate white meat by suction, centrifugal force, or vibration. Then the meat is pasteurized, which means it is heated to about 150 degrees F., and is canned. We tried some and thought the flavor was flattened by the processing. Try it for yourself. You can easily distinguish it from fresh crab meat. It's in a sealed can. One processor told us the meat will keep for a year.

Fresh crab meat comes in several varieties. The biggest lumps of meat and the fewest stray bits of shell are found in the containers marked "back fin." That's always the most expensive. Smaller pieces of white meat are found in the containers marked "regular" or "special." That's white meat other than the back fin meat, but may contain some claw meat, too. The claw meat is often packaged separately, in a third container marked "claw." It's a little darker and may be less expensive.

When you're making crab salad or crab imperial, the back fin meat is to be preferred. For deviled crabs, crab cakes, or crab soup, the regular and claw will do very well.

Is the sex of the crab a factor? When you buy crab meat in a can—sealed or unsealed—there's no indication of whether it came from male or female crabs or from both. Some people think there's a

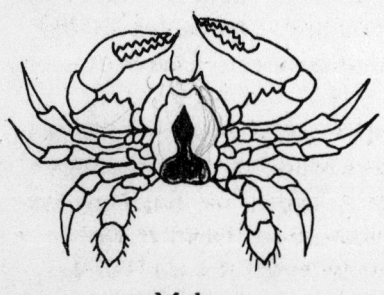

Male 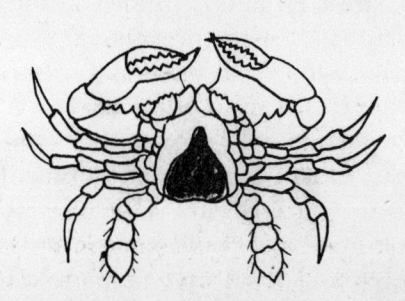   Female

slight difference in the flavor of the meat, and they prefer to buy male crabs when getting them live or steamed. We've eaten both and we detect no difference in flavor. Much of the meat that's packed in cans is from females. That's because the price of the female crabs is usually lower than the price of males at the docks where the watermen sell them. And that, in turn, is probably because the males grow larger and the larger crabs are in demand for eating as steamed hard crabs.

And now that we've talked about buying live hard shell crabs and canned crab meat, it's time to report that the third form in which crabs may be purchased is in the soft shell stage—live in season and frozen all year. Before buying any, you should try soft shell crabs in a good restaurant. But if you want to buy them for home use, there are a few places that carry them. You may find live or frozen soft shells for sale in seafood markets in the cities and suburbs. Food stores near the waterfronts where crabs are found sometimes carry them live in season. Another excellent source is those seafood firms who put hard shell crabs in shallow artificial ponds where the crustaceans can be watched in captivity and removed after they shed their shells in the process of growing. The crab that has shed his or her shell is a soft shell crab, going through the moulting process. In about three days the crab's new soft shell will harden and he or she will be a bigger hard shell crab.

If you ever have an opportunity to watch a crab extricating himself or herself from the old overcoat, it's a fascinating process, which the crab accomplishes with difficulty and determination. The shell splits and the crab backs out, tediously pulling each leg and claw out of its old armor.

Soft shell crabs are normally available in lower Chesapeake Bay from May until cold weather comes in the fall. When the water gets cold the crabs retire into a dormant stage, akin to hibernation. They dig themselves into the muddy bottom and rest there. In lower Chesapeake Bay, crabs are not only active again, but start to grow and moult in May. In southern North Carolina, they do the same thing starting in late March. So, the season for finding live soft shells varies with the locality.

Watermen and people in the crab business can tell when crabs are getting ready to shed their old shells. Those crabs, called peelers, can be distinguished by a touch of color on the next to last segment of the back fin. The color is pink at first, turning red before the peeler wiggles out of his or her old shell. It's difficult to find that "red sign" until you're quite familiar with crabs. So, leave that to the waterman and buy your crabs from him, or from a dealer.

And if you decide to try soft shell crabs at a restaurant, you will often have a choice of having them fried or sauted. We much prefer to have them sauted.

2. How To Catch Crabs

One of the many pleasant aspects of crabbing is that people rarely lie about the size of the crabs they have caught, although they may exaggerate the number, or the time it took to catch them.

"Went down to Quaker Neck yesterday and caught two bushels of crabs in an hour and a half," a fellow said.

We figured he was only lying about the time, not the volume. He was using a trot line baited with salted eel and he could have done about what he claimed, on a good day. Crabs aren't like fish—someone said the fastest growing creature in all of nature is the fish—from the time an angler catches it until he tells about it. No, crabbing isn't like fishing. Ernie Ford said fishing is just a jerk at one end of the line waiting for a jerk at the other end. We don't feel that

way about fishermen, despite the
fact that many of them don't enjoy
eating their catch. And that's a pity.
Few amateur crabbers—except for
children—are trying to round up a
basket of crabs just for the sheer
enjoyment of it even if it's a pleasant
occupation. They're looking forward
single-mindedly to the feast.

Before you go crabbing, you
should resolve to handle the live
crabs with your fingers as little as
possible. When transferring an individual crab from one place to
another, use a long handled tongs and let the crab try to bite that,
rather than your fingers. Crabs have speed and dexterity combined
with remarkable sight in all directions. If you ever have to pick up a
live crab by hand, grab his shell at the rear, between the two back
fins. That's the only place that's out of the reach of the claws, which

are amazingly maneuverable.

Catching blue crabs is a seasonal activity, limited by two factors: the habits of crabs and state laws. In general, you catch them when they are swimming around in tidal rivers, bays, and sounds connected to the Atlantic Ocean. You may catch them by using a net, a baited line, a crab trap, or, with certain limitations, a trot line, or a crab pot.

For amateurs this is a warm weather activity. That does not mean that crabs can not be found in their habitat in winter. In Virginia, the professional watermen catch crabs in winter by scraping them out of the mud. That explains in part how some restaurants are able to offer hard shell crabs in the cold months and why these crabs occasionally have a muddy taste. The rest of the explanation is that the restaurants get crabs from the warmer states, particularly Louisiana.

Crabs generally prefer salty water. They do come to the brackish waters of the upper Chesapeake Bay, but often not until August. If you want to go crabbing and aren't sure where the little beasts are, your best bet is to ask or watch the natives along the waterfront, or talk to people in bait and tackle shops, or places that rent row boats. Lower Chesapeake Bay and the coastal resorts of Delaware, Maryland, and Virginia have a longer crabbing season than the upper Chesapeake Bay, where we live in the summer. And North Carolina has a still longer season.

Bait

Crabs like to eat many things. Anything they like, that can be attached firmly to a line, can be used as bait to dangle in the water, such as chicken necks, backs, or wings. The professional watermen will call you a "chicken necker," but you have to expect that the professional will speak disparagingly of the amateur no matter what bait is used.

Fish heads also make good bait. You can get them free from fish markets. If you're a fisherman, save your fish heads and freeze them for use later as crab bait. Another excellent bait, with more lasting power than the others, is salted eel. Waterfront bait shops sometimes handle it; so do some commercial fishermen around Chesapeake Bay who put out eel traps. You have to inquire for it locally. We buy it by the pound from a fisherman at Georgetown, Md. It comes whole, and you cut it up into pieces about three inches long, which can be tied on a line.

Are you going to ask what kind of string to use for a hand line? Well, use white cotton cord, strong enough so that you can't break it by hand, or anything similar that you have. Suitable cord can be bought at the same hardware and general stores that sell crab traps and nets. Get something stronger than kite string.

And now for the technique of catching crabs by using a baited hand line and net. Obviously, go where the crabs are, and where you can approach them from above the water by operating from a pier, a bulkhead, a bridge, or a boat. Stay on a sure footing and avoid boats unless you know how to handle them and how to act in them. If you're not familiar with small boats, and a pier is not readily available, find a friend who is and get him or her to show you what you need to know on the water. If you're thinking of going out on Delaware Bay, first find out about the current.

You can crab from any kind of boat with an open cockpit. For this activity, a small runabout or a rowboat is best because you're close to the water and therefore don't have to dip your net very far.

If you are fortunate enough to own a small boat that you can trailer or cartop to some river or bay where you've heard the crabs are fairly plentiful, load up your lines, nets and bait and go there. It's as much fun as going fishing, and very similar. You have the dual pleasure of being out on the beautiful water and of gathering food from the sea. If you're in a place on the East Coast where there are no crabs, or very few crabs, the place to go is to the Delmarva Peninsula or further south. The further south you go, the longer the crabbing season. Try any of the rivers and bays. You don't find the blue crab in the surf, although some other crabs do swim in the surf and get washed up on beaches—in North Carolina, for example.

All right, let's go crabbing.

What you need, besides the bait and some lengths of line, are weights to pull the line to the bottom and a crab net. You can buy lead weights at a fishing tackle shop or use an old bolt or a rough stone that can be tied at the end of the line. Put the weight at the very bottom of the line and then tie on the bait a few inches from the end. No fancy knots are required. A simple overhand knot or half hitch—the first step in tying a bow for shoelaces or a package—will be sufficient to hold a piece of salted eel or a chicken neck. An overhand knot will come apart easily later when you have finished crabbing.

A net for crabbing is not something you can readily make. Simply buy one at a tackle shop or hardware or general store. Nets can be had with handles of aluminum or wood; either will do. Extra long-handled nets are also available. The normal length is better for crabbing from a boat or most other places; use a long-handled net only in places where you have to stand or sit relatively high above the water. We use nets with cotton mesh. It rots in time, but can be replaced. There are also nets with wire mesh. Either type will do with hand lines, but the wire mesh is preferred for trot lines, as you'll hear later.

To attract crabs, dangle the bait in the water with the weight touching the bottom. It's not necessary to hold the line by hand as you do with a hand fishing line. It can be made fast to anything that's available—a post on a pier, or part of the gunwale on a boat. Bait several lines and put them overboard at different places. The procedure is to go to one of your baited lines and pull it up very slowly. You may be able to feel a crab pulling at the line, but sometimes you can't. In any case, it's wise to pull the line slowly and cautiously until you can see the bait. Don't pull it out of the water.

When the bait comes into view, if there's a crab working on it, stop pulling up the line when the crab is about a foot below the surface. It's time for the net. If you're working alone and right-handed, take the bait line in your left hand and the net in your right hand. Lower the net very slowly to the water, then suddenly dip down and scoop up the crab and bait while pulling the line up a little further.

You may miss some until you get the knack of it because crabs will let go and swim away fast when they see the net coming at them. But after a little practice, you'll know how to insert the net and how far to pull up the line.

When two people are working together, one can handle the baited line while the other does the netting. If you're using a light runabout or rowboat, don't stand up in the boat. Do your crabbing in a sitting position. The reason, or course, is that a light boat can be capsized easily by being unbalanced. Similarly, two people occupying a light boat can't both crowd one side without risk of turning over.

You may prefer to put the net in the water before testing the line by pulling it up to see if you have a crab. Using that technique, you can try moving the crab and bait over the net before you swiftly swing the net up to scoop the catch.

Since you have to pull the line up many times, you will want to do the crabbing in water that's not too deep. We try to operate in water four to eight feet deep, but you can try deeper water if you have the patience.

An improvement in the simple cotton hand line can be made by attaching a piece of stainless steel wire at the end to hold bait that can be pierced rather than tied on, such as a fish head. Use a piece about 18 inches long and also find a piece of plastic tubing with an inside diameter just sufficient to hold two pieces of the stainless wire.

After attaching one end of the wire to the crab line, put the plastic tube on the wire near the same end. Pierce the bait with the wire and then put the free end through the tube to make a loop. Finally, attach a weight to the line. A good way to do that is to use a swivel out of a fisherman's box.

If there's no stainless steel wire handy, use a coat hanger. And if there's no plastic tubing, twist the ends of the wire together to form the loop after you have the bait on.

When you put out several baited lines, the procedure is to test each one occasionally—not every minute. Take your time. Enjoy the air. See how the crabs are biting. Adjust the time you take to make the circuit among the lines by the results you are getting. After about 20 minutes if you have seen no crabs, do something else for a while and try again later.

Opinion varies on when is the best time to crab in relation to the tide. Some people say crabs are hungry all the time, like teenage boys. In crabbing from a pier, we think we get best results when the current is running just before and after the high tide. But try crabbing any time you wish. And don't worry about the phase of the moon. When crabs are in the area where you're trying to catch them, they seem to be ready for tasty morsels regardless of whether the moon is waxing or waning. They move with the tide. The current may bring more of them into the range of your bait than still water.

Crab Traps

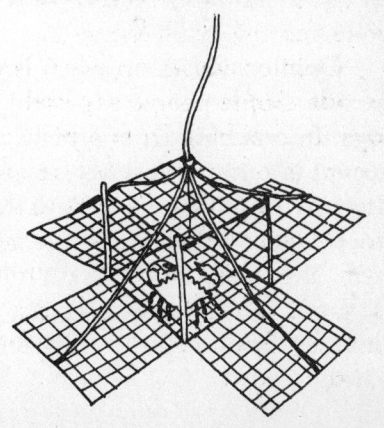

Catching crabs on a hand line is very satisfactory, but it does take a modest amount of skill in using the net. Using a collapsible crab trap, on the other hand, requires virtually no skill, and is less a sport. But it often catches dinner. The usual crab trap is a box made of wire mesh. Its sides—usually four—are hinged to the bottom. The contraption is rigged up with strings attached to the tops of each of the sides. These are attached to a single cord the crabber holds. When the trap is lowered to the bottom the sides flap open, baring the trap's mesh base with bait attached. A jerk on the string by the crabber quickly pulls the sides to their closed position and traps any crab who has ventured onto the base to check out the bait. The crabber periodically hauls up his trap to see if a crab has been caught. Or perhaps two at once. It's a beautiful system, when the crabs are there.

The procedure is delightfully simple. Tie the bait securely to the base or bottom of the wire box, using cord or wire. Chicken necks, backs or wings, fish heads, or whole fish can be used. Then hold the line while you drop the box into the water and lower it to the bottom, as with the hand line. Be sure to let out some more line so that the sides are open. Then relax. Give the crabs time to find the bait. After a few minutes, jerk the line firmly to close the trap, pull it up and see what you have.

If you have a crab, empty the trap by letting one side open and shaking out the crab into a basket, bucket, or other container.

When crabbing with either a hand line or a trap, you'll need such a container to carry your catch. In trying to empty the cotton mesh net, have a little patience. The crab will hang on until he sees where he's going and it helps to let him touch the bottom of the container where you want him to rest. Don't use fingers to get the crab to unlock his hold on the net—you'll be bitten. We take along a pair of metal tongs to use in picking up the crabs to measure them for legal size, sort them out and return to the sea those we can't keep. We tell them to grow up and come back later. The tongs are also excellent for convincing a reluctant crab to let go of the net or to get back in the basket.

If you are crabbing from a pier or bulkhead, it's prudent to tie the basket or bucket to something firm to keep it from being kicked overboard in the excitement.

We find that box traps work pretty well. Some are three-sided rather than four-sided. They're satisfactory. It doesn't seem to matter to the crabs, so it doesn't matter to us.

Crab Pots

Commercial crabbers get most of their crabs in crab pots and that's without doubt the most efficient way to catch them—if you can do it legally where you intend to crab. There are restrictions on the use of pots in several of the states; in some it is difficult or impossible for non-residents to use crab pots for recreational crabbing. These rules will be explained a little later in the section on state laws.

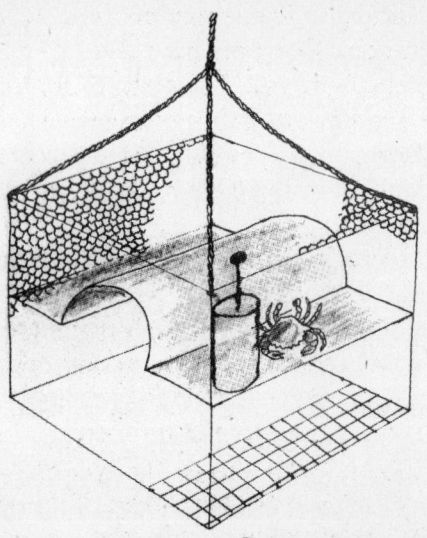

The crab pot resembles a trap in that it is a box made of wire mesh. But that's where the resemblance stops. The pot is much larger, its sides are not hinged, and it's made of zinc-coated wire that looks like chicken wire (but is not) rather than the small mesh used for traps. The pot is nearly a cube. The top and bottom are usually about two feet square and the height is a few inches less. It has openings big enough for a crab to enter. Each opening is at the wide end of a mesh funnel the crab can go through. There may be two, three or four such funnel-shaped entrances. Our pots have two. The inside ends of the funnels are flattened ellipses. The crabs swim into these entrances because they are heading for bait placed inside the pot in a cylindrical container of finer mesh. The pot also has a mesh partition separating the top section from the bottom, and this partition has two funnels opening from the bottom.

After a crab swims into the bottom of the pot and helps himself to some of the bait, he finds it mighty difficult to get in just the right position to go out through the narrow end of the funnel even though he came in that way. In looking for a way out, the crab is very likely to go into the wide openings of the funnel-entrances to the upper part and to end up there.

When we pull up our pot, on a good day, we usually find crabs in both the upper and lower compartments. We usually find males only, because the females do not roam in large numbers in the brackish waters where our pier is. We have checked our pot many times without immediately removing the crabs, and we've found that very few escape. The pot is a simple but very effective device, with no moving parts. However, it is not easy to make.

The beauty of the crab pot is that it operates unattended. Once you put the baited pot in the water, you can leave it and come back later at your convenience. Commercial crabbers set out large numbers of them attached to marked buoys and make the rounds each day, emptying and rebaiting the pots.

We keep a pot working at the end of our pier and usually check it each morning and late afternoon for a close-to-effortless harvesting of the best food the sea offers. With commercial crabbers, however, there's a great deal of hard work in pulling up the pots, shaking the crabs out, sorting them, putting in new bait as needed, and hauling the crabs to market. We salute them while catching only enough crabs for our own household.

Fish heads are our favorite bait, when we can get them free from the fish market and from fish we catch. We try to keep a few in the freezer.

There's not much of a trick to shaking the crabs out of the pot. One section of the top opens for that purpose.

If you can legally use a crab pot, the first chore is to find where to buy one. We've never seen them in stores. The last one we bought came from a fellow who makes them near Fenwick Island, Del., not far from Ocean City, Md. There's also a maker in Gratitude, Md., near Rock Hall, and one at Crisfield, Md. The way to find them is to go to crab country—particularly the Delmarva Peninsula—and ask the watermen at the docks, inquire at hardware or general stores, or look around for stacks of crab pots in a yard. Those stacks and a roll of what looks like chicken wire are the signs of a maker of crab pots. Before you rush out to buy one of these ingenious contraptions, check the section on the state laws.

Occasionally the bay supplies us with bait in the crab pot as an extra dividend. We pull up the pot from the murky water to see what Mother Nature has provided and are astonished to find a nice catfish or perch has either wandered into the enclosure or has become wedged in an opening of the steel mesh. Maybe it's so cloudy down there the poor fish can't see where they're going. If you do happen to catch a catfish in this way, put on a glove to handle him. And if you catch one big enough, eat it yourself—they're excellent. The crabs will be content with other fare.

The Trot Line

Many watermen use trot lines to catch crabs in volume, and so do some amateurs who crab frequently and have the space to keep the messy equipment. A trot line can be pictured as a very long line with many baits. The baits—usually salted eel—may be tied directly to the main line or to a series of auxiliary lines spaced along its length.

A trot line can be any length that's convenient. Usually it's at least 100 feet long. It can be of any material, but has to be strong enough to withstand a fair amount of tugging. Cotton cord one eighth of an inch thick will do.

To set up a trot line you will need, in addition to the length of cord, enough baits to attach every three feet or so, plus two buoys and two anchors. The buoys can be plastic bottles. The rig is made up by tying one anchor to one end of the line and then fastening a buoy, leaving enough room between the two so that the buoy will float at high tide where you want to put out the line. Measure out the desired length of line and put a similar arrangement on the other end—a buoy followed by an anchor. The entire rig, with baits attached, can be coiled and put in a barrel or tub and covered with heavily salted water.

The trot line is best used with a motor boat with low freeboard, although it can be used with a rowboat, a canoe, or in shallow water without a boat.

Let's say we're going to do some crabbing with a trot line and a rowboat with an outboard motor and that we have a two-person crew. First, we select the place we're going to try our luck and skill. We prefer an area where we can put out the line across the current rather than with it, and where the water is about six feet deep.

First we throw out the anchor and one buoy, then we slowly pay out the baited line as the boat moves along, making sure the line does not get caught in the propeller. When we come to the other buoy we stop the boat to drop that buoy and the second anchor. The anchor, of course, need not be a boat anchor. A piece of iron or anything heavy enough to stay in place will do.

Now we pause a few minutes, as with hand lines, to give the crabs a chance to gather at the baits, and we're ready to make our first run from one end of the line to the other, between the buoys. While one person steers the boat slowly, the other crabber picks up the baited line and lets it pass across one hand while holding the crab net in the other. The procedure is like using a hand line, except that the line comes to you without your pulling it up. You have to act swiftly to scoop up any crabs that are holding on to the baits. They must be scooped before the baits come up out of the water or they'll disappear. It takes some practice for both partners to do their job. And it requires speed and dexterity to scoop up the crab, let him drop into your basket and have the net ready for the next crab.

The best net for this purpose is one with steel mesh rather than soft twine.

An improvement in the equipment for running a trot line is to rig up a roller outside the gunwale of the boat, so that the baited line will roll up out of the water as the boat goes forward from one buoy to the other. Then the crew member with the net can put his full attention on scooping crabs and will not have to handle the line.

If the anchors are heavy enough, a lone crabber working a trot line can pull himself along the line in a light boat. There are other variations on the use of a trot line. One end can be attached to a pier rather than an anchor. Both ends can be attached to posts.

When crabbing is finished for the day, the trot line is coiled and put in the barrel, tub or plastic bucket. The eel baits are sprinkled with salt and the whole rig is covered with an old piece of canvas or other material.

Netting And Baitless Crabbing

It is also possible to go after crabs with no bait and nothing but a net and something to put the captives in, like a basket floating in an inflated tire tube and tied to your waist. One way to operate is to walk in shallow, fairly clear water where crabs are plentiful. You move very slowly, look carefully, spot a crab, and scoop him with the net.

You may catch hard shell crabs that way, or soft shells waiting for their new shells to harden, or you may find some doublers—crabs in the process of mating. It's not easy; crabs are fast at retreating. But it can be done. If you try it, be sure to wear sneakers with good soles and uppers because the sandy or muddy bottom is not guaranteed to be free of glass. Also, a crab you don't see may take a peck at your toe.

One of the major difficulties with this method of crabbing is that the places crabs are likely to be plentiful are the same places where the water is salty enough to be favored by sea nettles. They're a kind of jelly fish, prevalent in Chesapeake Bay from Rock Hall southward, that sting you on contact. We *have* seen men walking cautiously in water up to their knees along the banks of rivers of the Eastern Shore, including the Wye River, avoiding the nettles and slowly filling their baskets with crabs. It may be that Eastern

Shoremen have a special ability to dodge the sea nettle or to tolerate the stings. We don't recommend that method; when the sea nettles begin to appear, we don't compete with them for the use of the water.

It is also possible to net crabs from a boat, particularly a shallow draft boat that can venture into marshy areas. Among the grasses of such areas, you may find crabs who have gone there to shed. If you're lucky, you may find some soft shells this way. Netting crabs from a moving boat is called skimming.

There are times and places when you can catch crabs from a pier with a net and no bait. Places where the water is clear and you can see the crabs resting on the bottom lend themselves to this method. The upper Chesapeake is unfortunately too murky for that technique, but we have seen it done in a "salt pond"—an inlet from the sea—in Rhode Island. In that state, however, crabbing is for residents only.

The strangest method of catching crabs we ever heard of is called "jimmy crabbing." You do it by catching a good-sized male and tying a string onto one of his back fins. You put the crab back in the water and let him swim around and find a female ready to mate. The male will cradle the female. Then the couple can be pulled gently in by means of the string and dipped up in the net. When the female is removed, the male can be put out again to attract another. This can be done only in very salty water and when the girls are intensely interested in the boys. This occurs in May in the lower Chesapeake. The females caught this way will be ready to shed and become soft shell crabs. It's not a technique for beginners, and the season for it is short.

While crabbing is mainly a daytime activity, it is possible to catch the crustaceans at night. Some people go to a pier or out in their boats and use a flashlight. The light, played on the water actually attracts the curious crabs. The idea is to get them to swim within reach and scoop them up in the net. The trouble with this system is that the same light that attracts crabs attracts insects in greater volume.

It is also possible to gather crabs in a long net or seine. A net about four feet wide and about twenty-four-feet long, with poles at each side, is used in water up to about five feet deep. This of course involves walking into the water and subjecting yourself to the sea nettles, if they've taken over the territory.

Legal Sizes

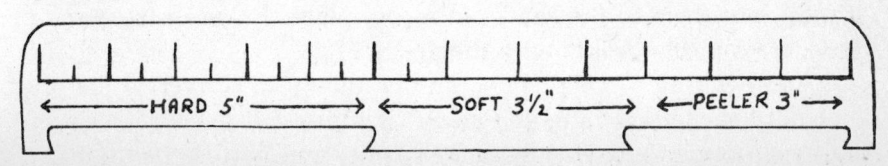

Regardless of how you catch your crabs, remember that you may keep only those that are of legal size and must promptly return to the water those that are too small. Give them a chance to grow up. It's a good idea to have with you, when crabbing, a ruler or stick marked with the legal sizes. In six states (Connecticut, Delaware, Maryland, Virginia, North Carolina and South Carolina) the legal minimum size for a hard crab is five inches, measured from tip to tip of the shell. A lot of crabs seem to measure 4¾ inches and that may strain your conscience.

Maryland's Department of Natural Resources gives out a "fish and blue crab ruler" made of plastic. It has the legal sizes marked on it in calipers fashion— five inches for the hard shell, three and a half for the soft shell, and three inches for the peeler, which is about to become a soft shell and grow.

For more details on legal sizes in the various states and their other rules, see the section on state laws.

The Live Box

Once you have caught crabs you can keep them alive in a cool place in a basket or ventilated box. Although they are creatures of the water, crabs can survive on land if they don't get too hot and dry. So, put them in the shade, in a cool place. Put some seaweed or damp grass in the basket with them.

Another way to keep crabs, and gradually to convert some of your hard shelled crabs to soft shells, is to use a live box. This is simply a wooden box with wire mesh sides and bottom and a mesh door at the top. You put the crabs in the box, lock the door and put the contraption in the water, tied to a pier or bulkhead. If you want to get soft shells, you of course have to look at the crabs periodically and remove those that have shed. If you don't get them soon after they're out of the old shells, the other crabs will.

Child Labor—Bay Style

There's nothing like a gathering of grandchildren and their assorted friends to insure a supply of our favorite crustacean. Neighbors' grandchildren will do, especially if the neighbors have never learned to love the blue crab. Here's the formula:

On a cloudy August morning, or a cool, partly sunny one, when the water is uninviting for swimming, beachcombing has temporarily lost its charm, and the youngsters are getting restless, start assembling the crabbing gear. Bring out the hand lines and the crab traps. These devices lure the kids, who want to know what those crazy looking things are and how they work.

After a brief explanation and a promise to demonstrate, get the crab nets, a ruler and bait, parcel out the equipment among the children and the procession to the dock is ready to march. Usually, before you reach the water, at least one child has proclaimed that he really knows how to handle a net. You're lucky if he does. Most times, you'll need to spend at least ten minutes showing him how tricky it is to have the net in the right place at the right time to capture the crab who's pulling on the line. If he learns quickly, one of the gang will almost immediately become an instructor for another willing would-be netter.

It's a good idea to take time to explain the minimum legal size for catchable hard crabs, using the ruler rather than the eye to decide whether to toss a crab back to grow awhile or add him to ones in the bucket. Get the kids to gather some grass or seaweed, wet it, and put it with the crabs they catch.

After you have the children set up with hand lines and traps, you're free to get back to reading, sleeping, bird watching, picture-taking or whatever is more appealing to you than sitting on a pier waiting for the next crab to bite or to be caught in the trap.

Children, on the other hand, seem to find special pleasure in the kind of pier-sitting that crabbing requires. They're very good at keeping themselves amused while bragging about their prowess, arguing about the length of a not-quite-legal crab, lording it over less fortunate line-holders, sometimes offering helpful hints to others, taking turns at the crab traps, and being willing to relinquish a job or coveted position on the pier to do a turn at beachcombing or stone-skipping from time to time.

In a couple of hours, if the crabs are there, this recreation project will have produced a harvest ample enough to be converted into cocktail delicacies, a dinner casserole and maybe even salad for the next day's lunch.

One of the serendipitous delights of this youngster-crab combination is that, unless they are bay-born and bred, most children do not consider crabs edible in any form. They're only good for sport. It's interesting, too. We've never heard a parent insisting that a child eat up all the nice crab meat on his plate. On the contrary, it's unlikely that a child's plate ever gets a crab on it. The cultivation of a taste for the lovely blue crab is never encouraged in youngsters. Appropriate, even lavish, praise for the crabbers' industry and catch is in order, and:

"That's all right, kids. You don't have to eat them—enjoy your hamburgers!"

Crab Hygiene

Live crabs have delectable meat inside, but are likely to be playing host to bacteria on the outside of their shells. This is not great cause for concern, but is the basis for a few rules on hygiene in handling crabs.

The first is that cooked crabs and live crabs should be kept in separate containers, and the basket or bucket you use for the live crabs should be reserved for that purpose. Steamed crabs should be kept in clean containers which have not previously been used for live crabs.

Second, any surfaces that have had live crabs on them should be cleaned and also sanitized. That can be done by wiping them with a solution of two tablespoonfuls of laundry bleach in a gallon of water. Containers for live crabs can also be sanitized with that solution if you want to put them to some other use.

Third, if you touch live crabs with your bare hands, wash them well before handling steamed crabs. And, by the way, if you want to pick up a live crab without getting a claw bite, pick him up between his back fins. Or, better yet, pick him up with tongs or with a hand encased in heavy leather or rubber gloves. This warning is repeated to impress you, reader.

The Red Crab
We certainly do not draw any color line, and the red crab is welcome at our house along with the blue. The reason we prefer to talk about the blue is that an amateur can go out and catch a batch of those marvelous creatures using the simple methods we have described. But you can't catch a red crab that way. The red crab, a relatively new entrant in seafood markets and restaurants, is not a suitable quarry for the recreational crabber because he doesn't swim

around where we can reach him. The red crab hangs out in very deep, very cold water, and is caught by lobstermen and by a few commercial fishermen who go out on the ocean and drop large traps to great depths—1,200 to 6,000 feet.

Until recently the red crabs that got into lobster pots were thrown away as a nuisance—just as blowfish used to be before someone recognized they have sweet, tender meat in them. Now a firm that goes after red crabs has popularized them by calling them "Big Red," and you can get them in some seafood stores and restaurants in Delaware and Maryland.

The red crab is already red when found in his native deep waters, unlike the blue crab, which turns red after being steamed. The red crab, on being steamed, just maintains his bright color. Also, he's big in the eyes of a blue crab. He averages about a pound and a half each, and has a lot of meat for his size. The flavor is a little different from the blue crab, but you can use red crab meat in any crab recipe, just as you can use king crab, if that's what you have handy. But for amateur harvesting, you can forget the red crab just as you would the king crab, which comes from Alaskan waters.

The State Laws

Crabbing is an activity controlled by state laws. The laws aren't too complicated and no license is required if you're an amateur interested in rounding up some marvelous food from the sea for your own use, and not for sale. Commercial crabbing is subject to more complex regulations. If you sell any crabs, you're regarded as commercial. Let's look at the laws on recreational crabbing in the ten coastal states from Massachusetts to South Carolina. The chart shows the main points, and the material below more fully describes the rules, state by state. Let's go from north to south, remembering that the further south you go, the longer the season is likely to be.

The states have size limits and a few other provisions based on the stage the crab is in before and after shedding the shell in normal growth. The *hard crab*, of course, is the crab with the fully hardened shell, and is the crab we commonly see. The *peeler* crab is a hard crab with a fully developed soft shell beneath the outer hard shell. This is a crab getting ready to shed. The *soft shell* is one that has shed its shell recently. The *buckram* crab or *paper shell* is one whose new shell has become leathery, but is not yet quite hard. Avoid taking buckram crabs in Maryland. The *sponge* crab is a female carrying a mass of orange-lemon eggs on her abdomen, between the back fins. That mass of external roe is known as the *bunion*.

In seven of the ten states, no one is allowed to take sponge crabs or females from which the bunion has been removed. The three states that do not have that prohibition are Massachusetts, Virginia and North Carolina. South Carolina, the home of she-crab soup, does have that prohibition. The roe used in she-crab soup consists of eggs the female is carrying internally. The roe in the bunion is unsuitable for she-crab soup.

In **Massachusetts**, the season for catching blue crabs extends from April 2 to Nov. 30. No permit is required to take up to fifty crabs per day, but no pots or traps may be used. No minimum sizes are specified.

In **Rhode Island**, non-residents may not take crabs. Residents may crab with net, trot line, or hand line in the daytime from May through November. The minimum size for hard shell crabs is 4 1/8 inches. Egg-bearing females may not be taken.

In **Connecticut**, the season goes from May 1 to Nov. 30 and crabbing may be done by net, trot line or hand line. The minimum legal sizes are five inches for hard crabs and three and one half inches for soft shells. Egg-bearing females must be returned to the water immediately.

In **New York**, there is no specified season and only two restrictions: don't take egg-bearing females and in some areas don't take crabs by dredging. Since dredging is a commercial method of crabbing, let's forget it.

In **New Jersey**, no license is required for crabbing unless you are a resident of the state who wants to use pots. A resident, non-commercial crabber may get a license to use two pots and catch up to one bushel of crabs per day, but may not sell them. The usual restriction on female crabs applies. The size limit deals only with peeler or shedder crabs—they must not be less than three and one half inches. The only other restriction is that trot lines with more than ten baits may not be used, except in Delaware Bay. No season is specified.

In **Delaware**, no season is specified for non-commercial crabbing, and all methods may be used except that a recreational crabber may not use more than two pots and they must be marked with white buoys with black lettering. The lettering must be "N.C." (for non-commercial) followed by the initials of the owner. The usual prohibition on sponge crabs and females with the bunion removed is in effect. The minimum legal sizes are five inches for the hard shell, three and one half for the soft shell, and three inches for the peeler.

In **Maryland**, crab season goes from April 1 to Jan. 1. The limit for recreational crabbers is one bushel of crabs per person per day. You may catch them with hand lines, dip nets, skimming from moving boats, with a trot line up to 300 feet long, a seine up to fifty feet long hauled up in the water (not on shore) or with up to five collapsible traps. Up to two unbuoyed pots may be set at any privately owned pier or dock, or two unbuoyed pots may be set within 100 yards of and in front of any privately-owned shoreline property. You may use a light to crab at night. Don't take egg-bearing females. The minimum sizes are: hard crabs, five inches; soft, three and one half; peeler, three.

In **Virginia**, there is no specified season. Recreational crabbers may use hand lines, the dip net, and a single crab pot, and may take up to one bushel per day. Trot lines and traps may not be used. The minimum size for the male hard crab is five inches, but there is no minimum size for mature females and soft crabs.

In **North Carolina**, an individual may take hard crabs by the use of one crab pot at any time for personal consumption, but no boat may be used in the process. The minimum size for the hard crab is five inches. There is no limit on the catch, and female crabs may be taken with or without roe.

In *South Carolina*, you may crab at any time for personal use by means of dip nets and hand lines, and you may use two traps or pots. If they are left unattended, your name must be attached to a float. However, no trap or pot may be set within 100 yards of a public boat landing or launching area, or set so as to be left dry at low tide. A pot or trap may not be buoyed with a glass bottle, jug or metal can. You must get a license to use a trot line. Female crabs bearing eggs or having the egg pouch removed may not be taken. The minimum size is five inches.

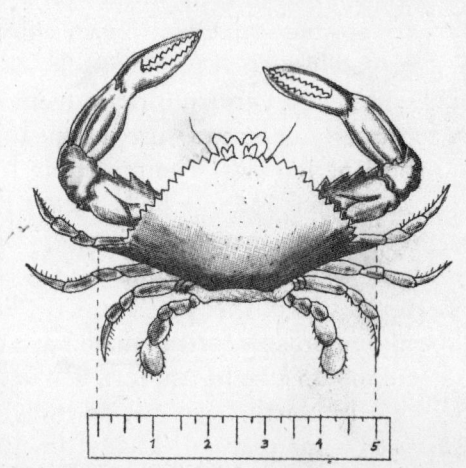

Summary of Recreational Crabbing Laws in ten states

State	Season	Limit	Hand Lines	Traps	Trot Line	Night Light	Pots	Females	Hard	Soft	Peeler	Other Rules
Rhode Island	May 1-Nov. 1	None	Yes	No	Yes	No	No	*	4 1/8			Residents only
Massachusetts	Apr. 2-Nov. 30	50	Yes	No		No	No	*	5	3 1/2		
Connecticut	May 1-Nov. 30	None	Yes		Yes		Yes	*				
New York	Anytime	None	Yes	Yes	Yes	Yes	2	*			3 1/2	Pots by residents
New Jersey	Anytime	None	Yes	Yes	To 10 baits	Yes	2	*	5	3 1/2	3	
Delaware	Anytime	1 Bu.	Yes	Yes	Yes	Yes	2	*	5	3 1/2	3	
Maryland	Apr. 1-Jan. 1	1 Bu.	Yes	5	300 ft.	Yes	1		5	3 1/2	3	No size limit on females
Virginia	Anytime	1 Bu.	Yes	No	No	**	No					
North Carolina	Anytime	None					boat		5			
South Carolina	Anytime	None		2	license		2	*	5			

*It is illegal to take females with eggs attached or from whom the bunion has been removed.

**Light may be used one hour before daybreak and one hour after sunset.

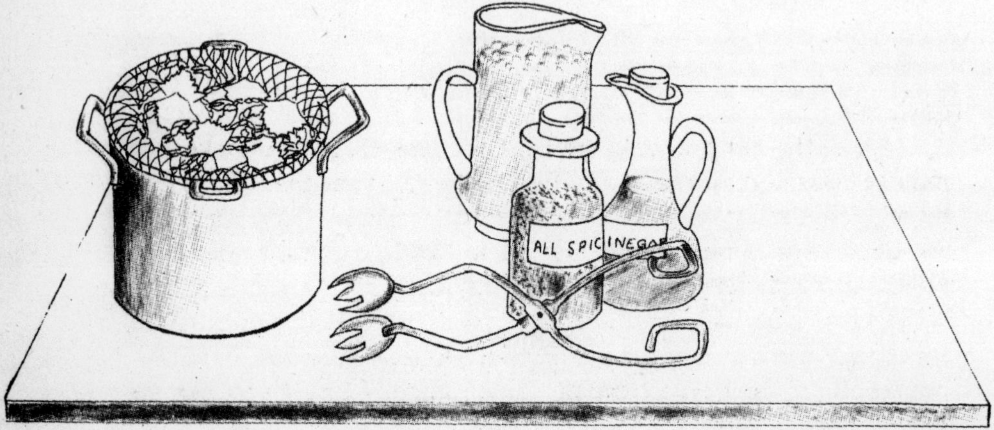
ALL SPIC
INEGAR

3. HOW TO STEAM AND EAT CRABS

Steaming

All of the hot and cold crab concoctions we like to make require cooked crab meat, and the best way to get that (aside from buying it) is to steam the live crabs you've caught. That's an important note worth repeating several times: the crabs *must* be alive when they are immersed in the cooking pot. If you are squeamish about this, try to reform your attitude. If you are not successful at that, appoint a less tender-hearted member of your household as chief crab steamer. If you already know you like the taste of the Chesapeake blue crab, you probably won't have too much trouble with the attitude-reform.

The chief cook in our family cannot bring herself to clean a fish, winces at stuffing a chicken, loses her appetite at the thought of cleaning one, and will not use any of the crab recipes that call for slicing a live crab in half. But, she merrily pushes those wriggling beasties into a steaming pot, without revulsion, convinced that the crab's mission is to give his life so that we all may feast on one of nature's most succulent foods.

For the steaming transformation you will need: a large, deep pot with a steamer insert to keep the crabs off the bottom and out of the liquid; long-handled tongs for handling the live crabs; smaller tongs or a grabber for removing the finished products. You will also need vinegar, spices, and, if you like, some beer.

For one dozen crabs, put water—or half water and half beer—one-inch deep in the pot. Add two tablespoons of vinegar. That's enough liquid; crabs have a lot of moisture themselves. Bring to a boil, under a tight lid.

Meanwhile, take the live crabs to the sink. Using the tongs, wash them well under cold running water. Transfer them, one by one, to the steaming pot, immersing them head first. They will be permanently subdued quite quickly. When the crabs are safely in the kettle, sprinkle them with two tablespoons of Old Bay Seasoning and a little salt, or with your own mixture of spices. Use a tight lid and steam the crabs for twenty-five minutes.

There are other methods for getting the crabs from basket to kettle. They can be immersed in very hot water, which will quell their fighting spirit so that they can be washed easily. We don't use that system, nor do we numb the crabs in ice water to quiet them for washing. We prefer the cold running water, because we want to know absolutely that each crab is alive and kicking when we begin the steaming.

If you are planning to pick the meat for a casserole or other dish, after the steaming let the crabs cool to the point where you are able to work with them without scalding your fingers.

In case a good sailing breeze has just come up, causing a change in the crab-picking plan, do the preliminary work: remove the "devil's fingers," the inedible innards and the upper shell, as explained later in this section. Then the crabs can be stored in the refrigerator in a plastic bag until the breeze has died and you're ready for serious crab-picking.

Seasoning

Old Bay Seasoning, a trademarked mixture which is called for in many Eastern Shore recipes, is a very hot collection of spices. Used in moderation, this product is a time-saver for the hurried cook, but it is potent, so be cautious as to quantity.

The list of ingredients on Old Bay's label includes: celery salt, pepper, mustard, pimento, cloves, laurel leaves, mace, cardamon, ginger, cassia, paprika and monosodium glutamate. No mention is made, of course, of the proportions, but if you get a very small pinch of it between your thumb and forefinger and taste it, you'll see how spicy it is.

We do use Old Bay because it *is* so easy, but we have also often steamed crabs using a bay leaf, mustard, celery seed and a couple of cloves, with a bit of cayenne and salt. Try your own combination, but use restraint.

About Picking Crabs

There is one big drawback to this business of making delectable dishes from the crabs we catch: the crab meat has to be picked. Once you've spent hours at this finger-wearying chore, we'll bet you will never again question the price of ready-picked crab meat. You may wince at it, but knowing how long it takes to fill a bowl with those tender lumps, you'll understand.

Nature's free gift of the beautiful blue crab certainly does reach us in a prickly package, and opening it and extracting the gem within is a tedious, time-consuming task. Experience does speed the job, however. Following the directions below will give you a good start on becoming a quicker picker.

If there happens to be an old school chum or a long absent friend among the guests who will share a feast of hard crabs with you, catching up on what life has been like in the long lapse between visits makes a great crab-picking accompaniment. Watching a special television program that one might otherwise feel guilty about spending hours on is another fine thing to do while fingers are occupied with crab-meat extraction. The Watergate hearings were one of television's best gifts to us crab-pickers; Senate hearings make an educational diversion; a concert of recorded music is a satisfying obligato to the messy business.

Crab picking is an occasion when newspapers—lots of them—on the table are a must. The shells, cartilage, and other discarded parts can easily be gathered up and disposed of neatly in the paper.

The other thing you will need is a sharp paring knife. A cutting board and a nutcracker will be handy, but you don't absolutely need them.

And now a word about the kinds of crab meat we're about to get. Unless there is an enormous supply of crabs, we do not try to isolate the back-fin meat from the body meat, as the commercial pickers do. We don't end up with those large lumps the seafood markets offer, but it doesn't cost us their astonishing price, and there are tasty dishes to be made of unsorted crab meat.

Unless the meat of the lower claw is needed to get the amount of crab meat you've figured you need to make a dinner, keep the lower claws separate and prepare them as "crab fingers" for excellent cocktail snacks.

When the crab-picking labor is finished for the day and you're not going to use the meat immediately, cover the bowls of meat with sheets of plastic or fitted covers and place in a larger bowl or pan of ice as indicated earlier for the store-bought crab meat. We keep it in this manner for two, not more than three days. Probably we're conservative; we're also always crab-hungry and we have never had any problem using however much we are able to get.

Picking

Oh, crab meat's a wonderful treat,
The most marvelous food you can eat,
But you know you must work to extract
That succulent meat that is packed
In the pockets locked under the shell.
In subsequent pages we'll tell
How to do it; but first comprehend:
It's worth every hour you spend.
So, patiently pick with your knife,
And prepare for the feast of your life.

Eating Steamed Crabs

About that classic newspaper-on-the table style of eating hard crabs, favored by many crab houses: it's messy. There is no way to keep hands clean and dry in the process of extracting that luscious meat from the shells and discarding the inedible parts. For real crab lovers, the messiness is part of the joy of eating, but for the uninitiated, it is likely to be an unappetizing horror. There is no elegant way of having a crab feast, but there are modifications that we use, without destroying the mystique. Your own house can be the best crab house.

First of all, newspapers have their own special sort of messiness—printer's ink. We resent having the ink from yesterday's paper mixed with the crab and lemon-butter coating our hands acquire, so we have revised the table covering. We use paper towelling (buy a lot of it on sale in the Spring), with double thicknesses along the table. We serve those handy little wash and dry pads, along with a large supply of paper napkins.

Heap the hot hard shells on a platter; provide a large bowl or bag for discards.

If we have guests who have not been introduced to hard shell crab eating, who are apt to keep us from making our own feast by needing too many instructions, we open the shells just before serving and remove the "devil's fingers," the useless insides and the upper shell.

As we've mentioned elsewhere, in the crab houses where steamed crabs have star billing, they are served smothered with salt, red pepper and other lip-burners, so that it is always assumed that a pitcher of beer accompanies every order. That high seasoning is often put on the crabs *after* they are cooked. It not only overwhelms the crab's delicate flavor, but reduces crab eating to an excuse for swilling beer at a proper profit to the management. Beer is a fine accompaniment to steamed crabs—and so is wine—but let's remember to protect the main dish. Let's not drown it to extinguish fire-in-the-mouth induced by over-seasoning.

Friends who have eaten crabs at our house marvel at the sweetness of the meat, exclaim at its subtle flavor. If you have in the past inundated crabs with salt and cayenne, try doing it our way— you'll enjoy more crab.

We go to the crab feasts put on by volunteer fire companies to raise funds and we find they generally overdo the seasoning just as the crab houses do. We take a napkin and wipe it off.

So, don't add any seasoning after your crabs are steamed. Serve them up. Give each guest a small bowl of lemon-butter, made with the juice of one lemon mixed in a half pound of butter or margarine.

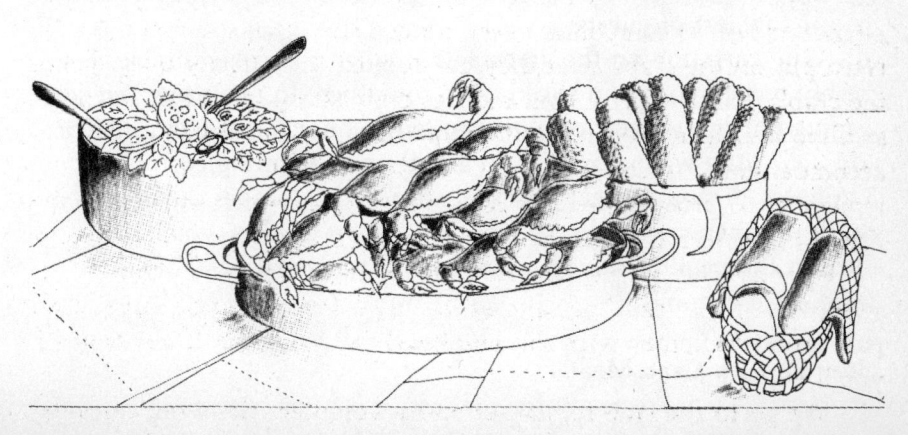

And give each guest a small, sharp, paring knife.

For the hard shell aficionado, as long as there are more crabs there is no need for anything else. We like the assessment of a friend who said a great many crabs, followed by a general hand washing and a mixed green salad and french bread adds up to a fine dinner for the fanciest of guests.

Our variation on the green salad, when they're available, is freshly picked corn and sliced fresh tomatoes. In preparing the corn, we line our large electric frying pan with inner husks from the corn, add very little water, bring it to a boil and steam the corn for about 8 minutes. If you can get both the corn and tomatoes directly from a nearby farmer, as we do, or from your own garden, you'll have them at the peak of flavor. Dessert with this meal has always seemed superfluous.

How To Pick Crab Meat

And now we're ready for the nitty-gritty of separating the meat from the shell and other inedible stuff inside so that you can eat what you've caught or bought. There are many brief descriptions on how to do that, but in our opinion they aren't specific enough. They're about as good as the cooking direction: "cook until tender." So, we're going to give a long exposition, one step at a time, in the hope that these directions can actually be followed by an uninitiated person faced with his or her first batch of steamed crabs. Later, we'll offer a shorter version. Get a paring knife.

Okay, the first step is to remove the claws. Not the four sets of legs, just the two big claws with the toothy pincers. If you're right-handed, which we'll assume, hold the steamed crab in your left hand with the claws forward and the one-piece shell at the top of the crab. Grab the claws, one at a time, with your right hand and pull them downward until they snap off. If any white meat sticks out of the broken claw joint, you're allowed to bite that off immediately as a small first reward for your labor. Set the claws aside.

Next, we want the shell off. That's done in two parts. Turn the crab over so that the apron on the crab's bottom is uppermost. Insert a knife near the top of the apron—of either the male or female which have differently designed aprons—pry up the apron, and pull it off.

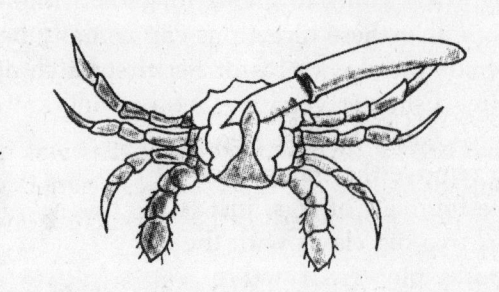

With the claws removed, the largest fins remaining are the back fins, which have flat surfaces for swimming. Hold the back fins with your left hand (you right-handers), put a finger of your right hand under the shell and flip it off. It doesn't require a lot of pressure. Don't discard the shell just yet. Two of the tastiest morsels you can

get from crabs are
sometimes hidden inside.
Put your knife into the
corners of the shell, inside
the points, and see if there
is some yellowish-brown
firm meat there. If a lot of
brown stuff hangs on, cut
that off, and just eat the meat that was inside the tip. It's marvelous.
But sometimes the crab has been netted at a stage where that meat
has not been developed. If it's there it's your reward for getting the
shell off.

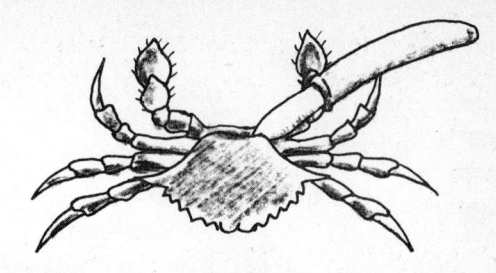

Now put the shell on the discard pile—which can be a mixing
bowl or a brown bag—and look at what's
left of the crab. It will be a more or less
round pad with four sets of legs attached.
On two sides of what we'll call the top,
you will see feathery, grayish gills, known

as the "devil's fingers." Tear them off or scrape them off, using your fingers or the knife.

We're at the point where there's just a layer of shell separating us from the white meat. We'll soon get that meat along with a little of the yellow stuff, which happens to be liver. Some people call it crab butter. It's very tasty. Save some when you get to it.

Next, hold the pad in your left hand with the back fins at the rear and the top still up. Break off or cut off the front portion, forward of where the "devil's fingers" were. That front portion is the nearest thing to a head that a crab has.

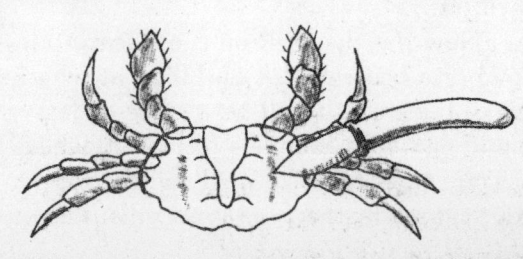

Still holding the crab in your left hand, look at the top. You will see a central channel with assorted things filling it, none plain white. That's the crab's insides. Push that material out with a finger or the knife, including any crinkly small items.

Now we have reached the stage where there are many techniques for proceeding to get out the luscious white meat from the pad. We will describe two quite different ones. In one, you leave the legs on for a while; in the other you cut them off as the next step. Commercial crab pickers use the latter system.

In the first technique, which we'll call Cy's method of enjoying steamed crabs, you break the pad in half along the central channel, leaving the legs on. Put down one half and take the other in your left hand. With the thumb and forefinger of your right hand grab the half-pad where the back fin is attached, putting the thumb on top. Press down with the thumb and up with the left hand to break off not only the back fin, but the part of the pad that's attached

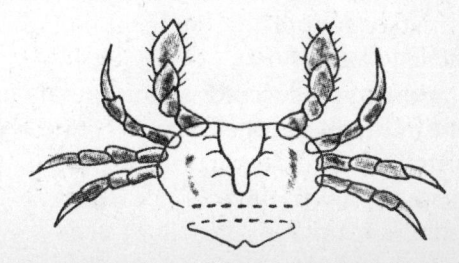

to it. Try to support the
top of the back fin as it
breaks away from the pad,
because inside the top is
the very best meat of the
crab—the famous back fin
meat. At first you will
probably find it falls out of the shell. That's okay. Put it in the bowl
where you're collecting crab meat, or eat it now. But after a little
practice—on your next six crabs—you will learn how to break the
shell while supporting the meat so that the back fin meat stays
attached to the fin.

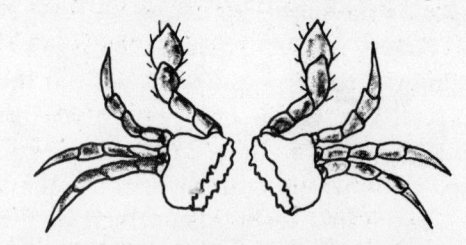

When you succeed in doing that, use your
knife to break the shell away from the upper part
of the back fin, the part nearest the pad. When that
is done, you will have Cy's crab meat lolly pop. Using the fin as a
handle, dip the lolly pop in your lemon-butter and bite off the meaty
top. Umm. That gives you the energy to go ahead with the work.

Next, proceed similarly with the other legs of the same half of the pad. Break each one off separately and try to pull the attached meat out of its shell compartment. Eat off the meat, or cut it off and put it in the bowl, or drop it in your lemon-butter container to eat later. Then break all the legs between the joints and squeeze them like tubes to see if there's enough meat inside to be worth the effort. Many people don't bother. We do. Okay, now we're through with the legs—discard the pieces—and go back to what's left of that half pad. Cut the half pad apart with your knife, cutting from side to side. The object is to lay bare the compartments containing the rest of the meat. Pick it out of each compartment with the knife. You can be as thorough as you like, or you can assume you got most of the white meat with the legs.

Then you're ready to go through the same procedure with the other half of the pad, starting with the back fin and proceeding to the legs. After that, get another crab. Later we'll do all the claws together, with directions below.

From this introductory exercise, you will have discerned that the meat in the body of the crab, which we call the pad, is locked in compartments at the top of the legs and claws. The trick, of course, is to get it out of those compartments with a minimum of the walls, made of shell or cartilage.

Now we're ready for the second technique, which we'll call Pat's method. It's more scientific and rejects the idea of pulling out the meat with the legs. On the contrary, in this method you start by cutting the legs off and putting them aside. Cut them off close to the pad. Even the back fin.

That leaves you with a fairly neat pad. The next step is to cut sideways through the pad to open up all the chambers where the meat is.

There are various opinions on how best to make that important cut. We think the best way is not a straight cut all the way through the pad from side to side. Instead, try not to bisect the back fin meat. Try cutting down at an angle of about thirty degrees (one-third of a right angle) from the rear top of the pad, so that your

knife will slit the top of
the back fin area and come
down at the center of the
second opening from the
back. That's the one next
to the back fin opening.
The object of this angled
cut is to get the back fin meat out whole—in big lumps. Make that
cut halfway through the pad, separating the back fin meat on one
side. Then place your knife at the center line of the four remaining
leg openings and cut through, parallel with the bottom, bisecting the
pad's one side. Then do the same on the other side. Open up the
pad, which has been cut into top and bottom portions. Use the point
of the knife to nudge, slide or pop out morsels of crab meat.

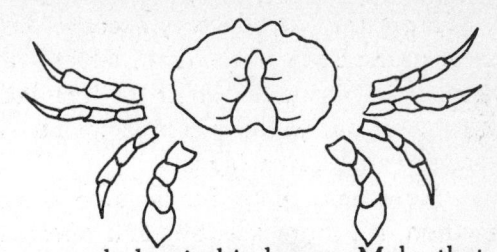

That's the speedier, more efficient technique, to be preferred
when you're picking crabs for consumption later, and you can also
use it for eating the steamed crabs immediately.

All right, if you're tired now, put the claws in the refrigerator in a plastic bag or covered bowl and get the meat out of them later. Whenever you're ready, read on about extracting the claw meat and making crab fingers.

First, though, having digested the long, detailed exposition on how to pick the crab's pockets, you may be ready for the promised short description of the same procedure. This is it (for a right-handed crab eater):

Hold the crab in your left hand, then break off the large claws with the right hand. Then pull off the top shell. Break off or cut off the legs. Scrape or pull off the gills. Remove the bottom flap. Remove the organs in the center part of the body. With the knife, carefully cut off the top right side of the remaining body, or inner skeleton, slicing from front to back. Remove any white meat that comes off with the shell. Then dig out the meat from the pockets along the right edge, starting with the back fin meat. Move your knife in a U-shaped motion to get that back fin meat; then pry up the meat from the smaller pockets. Then follow the same procedure on the left side of the body. Finally, follow the directions for getting out the claw meat.

How to Make Crab Fingers

Once the crab has been steamed, it is easy to break off the claws just by bending them too far, as we have noted. Similarly the two halves of each claw can be broken by hand by bending them further than the hinge will go. Then you have four pieces of shell with good chunks of meat inside. Put down that mallet. That meat can best be extracted with a knife and if you don't find that sufficient, get the help of a nutcracker.

Look at the lower part of the claw first, the part with the pincers. You will notice that one part is hinged like your jaw. You will also see, if you turn the claw over and over on any flat surface that the claw has a curve to it. One side is concave and the other is convex. Turn the concave side up and look for a dimple or slight depression in the shell near where the hinge is. Press your knife point into that depressed area, about a quarter inch back from the hinge. The shell is thin there and will crack. Once it has cracked, break off the non-movable part of the pincer, the part that's a portion of the main shell. Next take hold of the movable pincer and pull out the meat that's attached to it. If you're lucky it will come out whole and you will have a "crab finger"—a deliciously good bite of crab meat with half the pincer to use as a handle. Dip that crab finger in the lemon-butter or cocktail sauce, put the meat between your teeth and pull the meat from the cartilage that extends into it from the shell you're holding. A plate of those makes a wonderful cocktail treat. They can be bought in bags in some seafood stores; but now you know how to make them.

We get the meat out of the upper part of the claw by inserting the paring knife into the claw cavity and cutting the shell from the inside out. The easiest way is to use the knife as a lever, resting on one side of the tubular shell and cutting through the other. The nutcracker is also a satisfactory tool to use for the upper portion of the claw. Try to crack the shell and not squash it. The mallet is not a suitable tool; it tends to drive broken bits of shell into the meat, making more work.

Speaking of tools, the earlier references to a paring knife were not more specific because any sturdy paring knife will do. It should of course be clean. Maryland crab picking houses are required to have stainless steel knives—they use knives with both blade and handle of steel. That's not necessary for home use. We prefer a knife with a short blade and comfortable handle.

By the way, if you have never tried crab picking before, you may have assumed that some sloven had worked on the pound of back fin you bought and found not quite free of shell and cartilage. That's a good way to begin—being very, very careful.

It has always been surprising to us that, however meticulously we try to make sure not to confuse a bit of crab meat with a bit of cartilage, we always end up with some unwelcome invasion of shell or other unyielding material. Have you ever heard of a prize being offered for a pound of crab meat totally free of shell or cartilage? Anyhow, in the recipes to be given in the next section, the usual first line will be omitted. We will not start each one with "remove all shell and cartilage from crab meat." Rather, we'll assume you have been a fastidious picker, and will automatically check for any unwanted tatter of inedible bits.

And here's a final question to consider after you have picked your first batch of crabs. Now that you've washed and soothed your tired, stiff fingers, how much would *you* charge for one pound of crab meat?

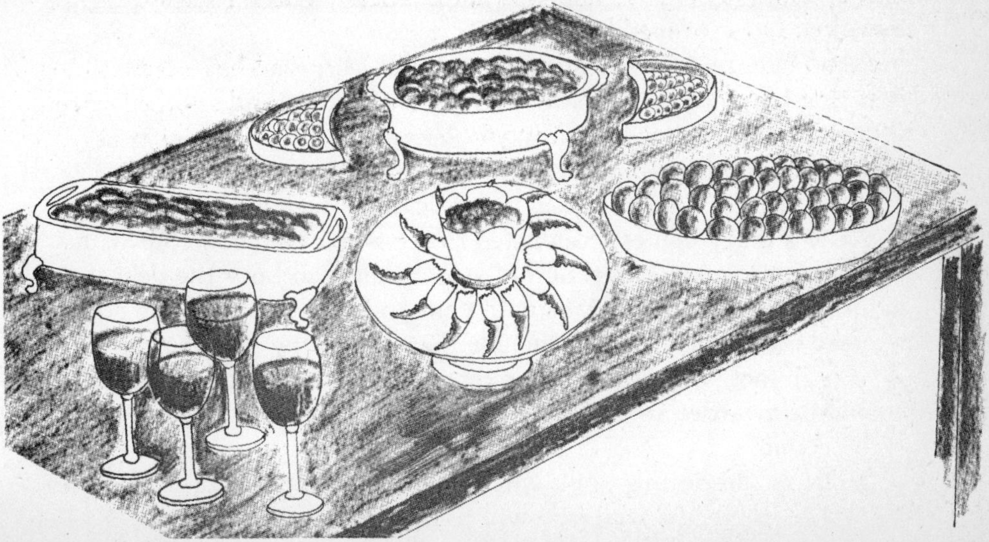

4. COOKING WITH CRABS

There are hundreds of recipes for preparing crab meat in many different dishes. Some of them are ridiculous, seeming to be the result of a crazy contest conducted to see who could come up with the most outrageous collection of strong spices to bury the delicate natural flavor of crab. Crabs with chili and corn flakes is one horror we read recently. We won't include that sort in the recipes that follow. In fact, we suggest the inventors of such disastrous dishes should be awarded several nips from the pincers of the largest jimmy crab around.

The recipes in this book will give you a great deal of freedom to improvise, which is what you will find yourself wanting to do if you are crabbing and never know how large the catch will be. On a really successful crabbing day—or two of them—you'll want a variety of ways to serve your treasure. Revising the daily menu (putting that beef back in the freezer), becomes the order of the day when crabs are plentiful.

Ours is the ad lib school of cooking. If we specify margarine, feel free to use butter, if you are not concerned about the amount of cholesterol you ingest. When our recipe calls for milk you may use half cream if you prefer a richer dish. In recipes where we feel cream is needed, we blink at calories and cholesterol. Be your own arbiter.

Because we are somewhat isolated from so-called civilization, where we catch, cook and eat crabs, we've made some of our finest culinary creations with good substitutes. We keep a supply of dehydrated onion, celery flakes, dried parsley, herbs and spices. And we try to have a large assortment of standard cream soups for concocting sauces. We also use non-fat dry milk and have weaned ourselves (for the most part) from cream, feeling smugly healthy and aiming for slimness.

Incidentally, crab is a very low calorie, high protein food. The cholesterol it contains we have convinced ourselves must be beneficial.

Another standby that is handy to have for many crab dishes is chicken stock, made on a rainy or windless day, when we can't go sailing. It can be de-fatted, poured into ice cube trays, frozen, and then transferred to plastic bags for storage in the freezer compartment. Hereafter, when a cube or two of chicken stock is mentioned in a recipe, you'll know what is meant. Fish stock can be stored in the same way, but will not keep as long as the chicken cubes. If making stock does not appeal to you, use one of the instant chicken bouillons to be found in the supermarkets.

But, if you just happen to be stewing chicken to make a salad for that mob you expect on the weekend, do let the liquid cook some time longer, after you have removed the chicken from the pot. Then, let the liquid cool, remove the fat, strain the stock and pour it into ice cube trays. (Of course you will have remembered to include celery, carrot, onion, parsley stems and leaves as well as a bay leaf, some cloves, peppercorns, and salt to the cooking water.)

You may indeed find it so handy to have chicken stock in such convenient form that you will get the resident crabbers to share their chicken necks, backs, and wings with the cook; then you can make stock without a stewing chicken.

Fish stock is also an easy cooking staple to make, and the main ingredient is, after all, free from the water. Use fish heads, tails, and bones. Barely cover with water. Add one or more celery stalks including the tops, chopped coarsely; one medium-sized onion, cut in four pieces; one small carrot; half a cup of vermouth; a quarter cup of parsley stems and leaves; two cloves and two peppercorns. Bring this to a boil and simmer for an hour. Strain carefully and use the ice cube tray method of freezing, then store in a plastic bag. A few cubes of this stock makes a good addition to many sauces and just might make a masterpiece of a crab soup you may originate some day.

Parsley is another of our favorite cooking accessories—such a tasty green, useful in many recipes. In our bayside retreat, it's hard to come by. We don't attempt to grow it, knowing that the rabbits would always be the greediest share-croppers. Often, when we do have a lovely, fresh bunch of parsley, we do not have a chance to use it all before it loses its crispness. Our solution is simple: never throw out somewhat elderly, limp parsley. Put it on a cookie sheet in a low oven (225 degrees), or a cooling oven after you've roasted or baked some food, and let it dry. Then crumble it in your hand and store it in a jar for future recipes—no need to get that store-bought dried stuff.

Crab Soups

For many years we've been pursuing crab soups up and down the East Coast, from lowly small town luncheonettes to elegant waterfront and city restaurants. We've spooned through hundreds of sad bowls full, only rarely finding a really excellent concoction.

The variety most often served around the Eastern Shore in Maryland is really a vegetable soup with a bit of crab tossed in. The tastiness of the product depends on how good the vegetable soup was to begin with. To us, this sort has always been disappointing.

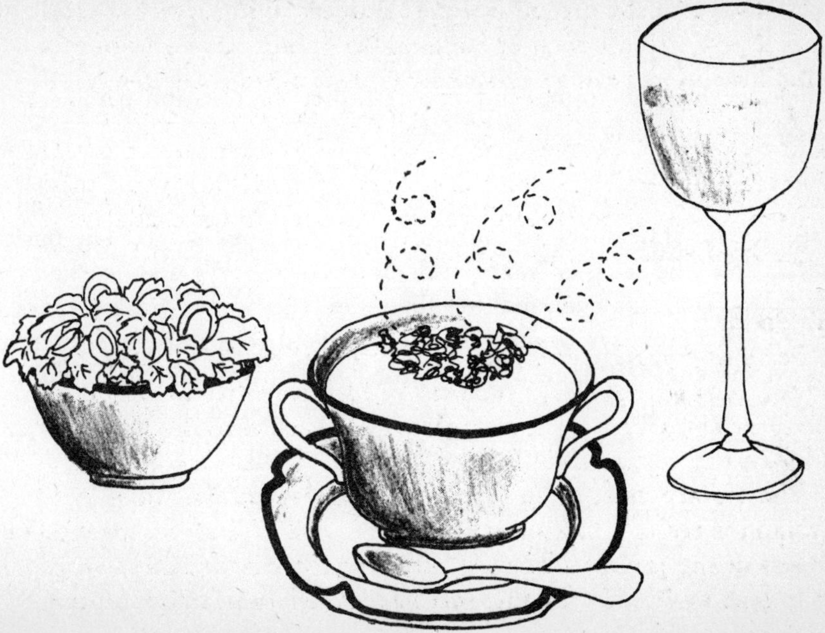

Deciding that we prefer a creamy crab soup, we've downed many miserably floury mixtures, masquerading as crab bisque, and have found some good ones. But the queen of all crab soups, we think, is she-crab soup. And among those, the creation we like best is by Henry's restaurant in Charleston, S.C.

After eating Henry's soup for four days, and raving about its quality, we were given a nugget of knowledge by the niece of the Henry who started the restaurant about forty years ago. The basic seasoning, she said, is "mace and sherry wine." We also learned that the same chef has been making their she-crab soup all these years.

Back home, we began creating beautiful soups, always including mace and sherry. Mace! What a word—what a spice! Not a club, nor the spray used to disperse unruly mobs, but a deliciously aromatic spice. It's similar to, but more flavorful than nutmeg. Mace is ground from the layer between the nutmeg shell and the outerhusk. For us, it is the perfect accent for crab soup.

Sherry for crab soup-making should be dry. If marsala is what you happen to have, it will do, but use less because it is sweet.

Here are two crab soup recipes, one assuming you have lots of time to cook and the second assuming you'd rather be out sailing and get home at the last minute for food preparation.

CRAB SOUP #1

- 3 tbs. celery (including some tops), finely minced
- 1 shallot or scallion, finely minced
- 1 tbs. water
- 1 1/2 cups crab meat (claw and body; not back fin)
- 2 cubes chicken stock *
- 2 eggs, hard-cooked
- 1/4 tsp. mace
- Dash garlic powder (optional)
- 2 tbs. parsley stems, finely minced
- 1/4 lb mushrooms, cut up
- 5 tbs. margarine
- 3 1/2 tbs. flour
- 3 1/2 cups milk
- 1/2 tsp. salt
- Dash cayenne
- Dash MSG
- 1/3 cup sherry
- Dash white pepper

* See page 84

While the eggs are cooking, melt one and one half tablespoons margarine in a small, heavy saucepan. Add very finely minced celery, parsley stems, shallot, and mushrooms. On medium heat, toss frequently for three minutes. Add one tablespoon water, cover, and simmer three to five minutes, and set aside. Heat milk and chicken stock to boiling. Meanwhile, melt remaining three and one half tablespoons margarine in a very heavy pot (we find the best is enamelled iron), and add flour. Mix with a wooden spoon on low heat for two or three minutes. Mixture will be frothy and bubbly. Add the hot milk and chicken stock mixture at once, stirring vigorously with a wire whisk so there won't be any lumps. Keep heat very low. Mash egg yolks well; mince whites. Add them and the celery mixture to the soup. Stir. Add the spices, sherry and crab. Stir carefully; simmer twenty minutes, and taste. This is where you're on your own. You can add minute portions of spices if you wish. As we said, this is the ad-lib school of cooking and only *you* know what pleases your palate. But remember, crab can be overwhelmed easily by too strident spicing.

Serve soup in warm bowls with freshly minced parsley on top. Crackers or melba toast are good accessories. With a large, tossed vegetable salad and some fruit for dessert, this is a deliciously satisfying meal for 4, or it makes a delightful first course for 6 to 8.

CRAB SOUP #2

This is the jiffy soup. Start cooking the eggs as soon as you arrive in the kitchen; hard-cooking them takes longer than anything else in the recipe.

- 2 eggs, hard-cooked
- 1 can cream of celery or cream of chicken soup
- 1/4 soup can sherry
- Dash cayenne
- Dash garlic powder
- 1 tsp. dehydrated onion flakes
- 1 can cream of mushroom soup
- 1 3/4 soup cans milk
- 1/4 tsp. mace
- Dash white pepper
- 1 1/2 cups crab meat (claw and body; not back fin)

Use a heavy-bottomed pot (enamelled iron is best) and mix soups, milk, and sherry with wire whisk. Add spices and crab meat. When soup mixture is smooth and hot, mash hard-cooked egg yolks and chop whites finely and add to soup. Taste before you add salt, since there is usually enough salt in the canned soups. Keep heat low, so soup warms slowly and flavors get a chance to blend. Let it simmer while you make salad.

You will find out by experimenting which canned product makes the best crab soup. We generally use Campbell's. Serves 4 to 6.

SHE-CRAB SOUP

In our kitchen we have a colorful little poster from Charleston, S.C., with this recipe for she-crab soup.

2 cups white crab meat and crab roe	A few drops onion juice
1 quart milk	1/4 pound butter
1/4 pint cream (whipped)	1/4 tsp. mace
Salt and pepper	1 tbs. flour
1/2 tsp. Worcestershire sauce	4 tbs. dry sherry

Melt butter and blend in flour. Add milk, crab meat, roe, and all seasonings except sherry. Cook slowly over hot water for twenty minutes. Add one half tablespoon warmed sherry to individual soup bowls. Add soup and top each serving with whipped cream. Serve hot. Serves 4 as a main course; 6 to 8 as a first.

(This recipe should tell you to blend the butter and flour until they are foaming and heat the milk before adding. Also, unless you live where you can get crab roe (as in Virginia or North Carolina), use two, mashed, hard-cooked egg yolks as a substitute.)

CRAB BISQUE #1

We think that crabs in almost any form are food fit for a king, but we have only recently learned that presidents favored them, too. Both George Washington and Franklin Delano Roosevelt liked to eat crab bisque. Here are a couple of recipes for that lovely soup. First, the low-calorie version.

- 3 cups milk (non-fat dry milk mixed)
- 1 small onion, chopped
- 2 cloves
- 1 tbs. margarine
- 1/4 tsp. salt
- 1 cup crab meat
- 1 stalk celery, chopped
- 1/2 cup (4 cubes) chicken stock
- 1 tbs. flour
- 1 bay leaf
- 1/2 tsp. Tabasco
- Fresh parsley, finely minced

Heat stock and milk to boiling point with celery, onion, cloves and bay leaf. Simmer for about fifteen minutes. Strain. Melt margarine, stir in flour with wire whisk for about four to five minutes, until frothy. Add hot milk mixture and crab meat. Simmer slowly, stirring carefully. Serve in hot bowls; garnish with parsley. Serves 4 to 6.

CRAB BISQUE #2

1/2 cup mushrooms, sliced
1/2 cup celery, finely chopped
3 tbs. butter
1 tbs. flour
2 hard-cooked eggs, sieved
Grated peel of 1 lemon
1 tsp. Worcestershire sauce
1/2 cup heavy cream
1 quart milk
1 tsp. onion juice
1/4 tsp. mace
Salt and pepper to taste
2 cups crab meat
1/4 cup sherry

Saute mushrooms and chopped celery lightly in 1 tablespoon butter. Cover, simmer, and set aside. Blend two tablespoons melted butter, flour, sieved eggs, lemon peel and Worcestershire sauce to a paste and put into very heavy pot (or top of double boiler). Scald milk and cream together; blend in onion juice and mace. Using wire whisk, stir into paste in heavy pot. Bring to boiling point, stirring constantly. Add crab meat, sautéed celery and mushrooms, and sherry. Heat slowly so that all flavors blend. Serves 4 to 6.

The second crab bisque recipe makes a much more delicious, and, alas, much richer soup. There are happy mediums that a resourceful cook can concoct. Our motto: taste frequently while preparing and add seasonings in small amounts.

There are other crab bisque recipes that call for dismembering live, uncooked crabs. We reject those.

How to Ruin Crabs or Somebody Else's Favorite Crab Dinner

The first time we ever ate crabs might very well have been the last, if we had not learned that there are other ways to prepare the blue crab. The clearest memory we have of that initial crab-eating fiasco was chasing very lively live crabs around our kitchen floor as, one by one and in twos and threes, they escaped the not-so-tight security of a deteriorating basket.

There were plenty, nay a plethora, of angry crustaceans that day, the result of an interesting crabbing trip made by two acquaintances who decided, very generously, to share their largesse with us. A young couple we knew had gone to Rock Hall in the days when it was possible, even easy, to walk into the water with dip nets and gather the plentiful crabs to fill as large a container as one happened to have.

Our crabbers had been deft and greedy and turned up at our house with the lavish results of their day's outing. We'd been advised to have a large batch of spaghetti sauce cooking, a supply of thin spaghetti and a pot in which to cook crabs.

There were problems. First, even the largest pot in our kitchen was too small for this introductory horde; they had to be cooked in three shifts. Second, no tongs we owned was long or strong enough to grab the crabs without having them grab us. It would have helped if we had known how to get hold of the crabs, but back fin was not yet in our vocabulary.

We finally steamed as many of those wily beasts as our pot would hold, by now having lost any enthusiasm for eating them, much less their uncooked comrades awaiting their doom in a sturdier container. And then our friends, the crabbers, said it was time to cook the spaghetti. Spaghetti? We had forgotten about that, and now began to wonder about the relationship between it and the crabs.

We found out. The idea was to throw cooked crabs, broken in half, not cleaned of inedible parts, into that fragrantly bubbling spaghetti sauce. We were brave and tried to act as though we were enjoying the incredible messiness of eating something that we regarded as an unsanitary invasion into perfectly good sauce. We did not learn that day what crab meat tastes like—the tomato sauce engulfed it totally. And so, dear reader, that is why we have never been persuaded to cook or eat crabs in any sort of tomato sauce.

The nearest we have come is to try crab meat dipped in that ubiquitous hot red cocktail sauce that nullifies the taste of any seafood. We thereby enforced our distaste for the crab-tomato combination.

So, if crabs and tomato sauce sound appealing to you after all that, you can readily find recipes. We can't recommend it.

Basic Sauces

Many crab meat entrees we like to make (and hundreds of variations you may create) require a basic sauce—béchamel, velouté, or white sauce—whatever you call it and however you modify or flavor it. If you do not already know how, learn to make it easily and surely.

The first thing to remember is to use a very heavy pot. In the dim days of mother's kitchen, a double boiler was used, but that is an unnecessary nuisance. If you didn't read the earlier remarks on this subject, we prefer enamel on iron or steel for a heavy pot, and have several casseroles which travel well from top of stove to oven to table. Heavy stainless or Pyrex will do, if that's what you have. Aluminum is not preferred, and do not use plain iron. The heavy pot is needed so that the roux—the flour and butter mixture—will not burn, and the sauce will not stick to the pan.

The next requirement for a good, smooth sauce that does not taste floury (ugh!) is low heat and a few minutes of stirring with wooden spoon or paddle until the butter and flour combination is frothy, but not brown.

The third and most telling point is heating the liquid for the sauce *before* adding it to the roux. If the liquid (milk, or milk, stock, and/or wine) is hot and you stir it into the hot roux with a wire whisk, the sauce will never be lumpy.

Béchamel sauce is made with milk. Velouté is made with stock. That is the strict definitive difference. But in our ad-lib tradition, we ignore this boundary and often use chicken (or fish) stock with milk; and sometimes we use vermouth as part of the liquid.

For every two cups of liquid, use about three tablespoons of flour, two of butter or margarine. Naturally, if you need a thicker sauce, use more flour. If you misjudge and get the sauce too thin, either cook the sauce longer until you get the thickness you want, or add a little paste of butter and flour and beat it into the sauce on low heat. An even easier, and just as satisfactory, way to make the sauce thicker is to stir in some cornstarch, mixed with water.

Now that you know the secrets of success of sauce-making, you need never be awed by recipes that require them and may even be ready to branch out and try your own seasoning additives to create new dishes.

CRAB MORNAY

2 tbs. butter or margarine
3 tbs. flour
1 1/2 cups milk
1/4 cup dry vermouth
2 chicken stock cubes (or 1/4 cup stock, or dehydrated chicken bouillon)
1/4 cup Parmesan cheese, grated
1/4 cup Swiss cheese, grated
1 pound crab meat
Salt and white pepper
2 dashes of mace

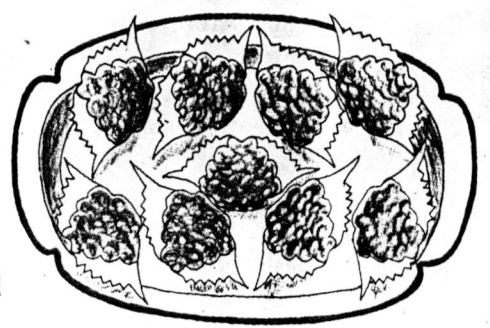

Melt butter in a heavy pan; add flour and stir on a low heat for several minutes. Heat milk, vermouth and stock to boiling; add all at once to the roux and stir with a wire whisk until smooth. This will take several minutes. Add the grated cheeses, continuing to stir with whisk until sauce is completely smooth. Add crab meat and stir gently on low heat. Taste and add spices.

Put in shells, ramekins, or casserole in 350-degree oven, with buttered crumbs on top. Bake about fifteen minutes, or until bubbly and light brown. Garnish with crisp parsley.

To make buttered crumbs, melt butter in small heavy pan and add fine bread crumbs until butter will not take any more. Serves 4.

CRAB MEAT DEWEY

We've never heard whether this is named for the admiral or for the governor, but either way it makes a delicious entree served with a tossed salad and, in the summer, with fresh, buttered lima beans. If mushrooms are easily available and you need to stretch this recipe, feel free to increase their amount. Mushrooms and crab meat complement each other very well, their delicate flavors blending beautifully.

3/4 cup mushrooms, sliced to retain the mushroom shape
5 tbs. margarine or butter
1 1/4 cups milk
2 cubes chicken stock
2 tbs. dry vermouth
Dash mace
1 pound crab meat, well-picked over to remove cartilage
1 tsp. onion juice
3 1/2 tbs. flour
Salt and white pepper
1/4 cup light cream

Saute mushrooms in one tablespoon margarine for a few minutes. Set aside. Heat milk, chicken stock, and vermouth to boiling. Melt two tablespoons margarine and saute crab meat for few minutes, tossing constantly. In a heavy pot, melt two tablespoons margarine or butter, add flour and stir on low heat until mixture is frothy (three or four minutes.) Add hot milk mixture to roux all at once, stirring constantly with wire whisk. When sauce has thickened, add crab meat and mushrooms. On low heat, re-heat whole mixture, adding cream a little at a time. You may not need the entire amount. Add salt, white pepper, and mace to taste. Let simmer for ten to fifteen minutes. Serve from large casserole or heated individual ramekins. Garnish with fresh parsley. Serves 4.

CURRIED CRAB ALMONDINE

1 pound crab meat
4 tbs. margarine
2 tbs. onion, finely minced (or 2 tsp. dehydrated onion)
1 medium Winesap apple, chopped
1/2 cup celery, finely chopped
1 tbs. good curry powder
2 tbs. flour
1 1/2 cups milk
1/2 tsp. salt
Dash or two pepper
1/2 cup toasted slivered almonds

In a heavy pot, saute onion, celery and apple in three tablespoons margarine or butter until onion is translucent. Add less than one tablespoon more butter, the curry, and flour. With wooden spoon, stir on medium low heat for at least three minutes. Heat milk to boiling point and add to curry mixture, stirring constantly with wire whisk until sauce thickens. Taste and add salt and pepper as needed. Let sauce simmer about fifteen minutes, stirring only occasionally. You may need to add a little milk or cream to get the right consistency. Then add the crab meat and almonds. Re-heat, stirring very carefully to keep the crab pieces from breaking up.

You can make the curry sauce earlier in the day and heat it up before adding the crab and almonds.

Spoon into greased shells and put under the broiler for a couple of minutes.

This is a deliciously tasty way to serve crab. We suggest you want to add less curry than the recipe calls for until you have tasted it, to make sure it's right for you. Serves 4.

DEVILED CRABS LOUISIANA

This is a perennial favorite that you find with many variations. The quality generally depends on the amount of crab meat. Here is a recipe someone brought us from New Orleans:

- 1/2 cup shallots (or scallions)
- Butter
- 1/4 cup brandy
- 1/2 tbs. Dijon mustard
- Enough béchamel sauce to bind the crab meat— about 1 cup
- 1 lb. crab meat (body and claw)
- Salt and white pepper to taste.
- 1 cup seasoned bread crumbs

Saute shallots in butter until they are transparent. Remove pan from fire and swirl with the brandy, adding a little of the mustard at a time. Add the béchamel gradually. Finally, combine crab meat

with this mixture. (You'll have to judge the exact amount of béchamel sauce needed to bind the crab, so add it slowly). Taste and add salt and white pepper if needed. Pour mixture into cleaned crab shells and cover each shell with seasoned bread crumbs. Dot each shell with butter and put under boiler until crumbs brown. Serves 4 to 6, depending on size of shells.

Crab shells can be cleaned up easily and used as natural serving dishes for this and other crab concoctions. The advantage, as in using a ramekin or piece of pottery in the shape of a clam or crab shell, is that each individual serving is in its own neat container.

To transform those messy looking shells into the most inexpensive ramekins, first scrub the shells well with a stiff brush. Then put them in a pot, add one tablespoon baking soda for each six shells, cover them with water, and bring to boil. Let simmer for twenty minutes. Dry the shells and there are your new dishes. Keep them clean—treat them as you would any ramekin. The greatest advantage is the replacement cost.

DEVILED CRABS MARYLAND

This one came from Annapolis. It has an unusual ingredient for this dish—sage.

3/4 cup milk
3 tbs. margarine or butter
2 tbs. celery, very finely minced
2 tbs. onion, very finely chopped (try half this amount, if you like)
2 tbs. flour
Dash lemon juice
1/2 tsp. dry mustard
1/2 tsp. sage
1 tsp. Worcestershire sauce
Dash cayenne
Salt and white pepper
1 egg, beaten
1 lb. crab meat (body and claw)
2 tbs. parsley, minced
Buttered fine bread crumbs

Heat 1/2 cup of the milk while you saute the onion and celery in margarine until they are translucent, but not brown. Blend in flour and stir on low heat until flour has a chance to cook a little. Mixture will be a little foamy. Add hot milk and stir with a wire whisk. Add the lemon juice and all seasoning except salt. Beat the egg in a bowl with 1/4 cup milk. Stir in a little of the hot sauce to the egg and milk mixture; then add the mixture to the sauce in the pot. Add the crab meat and parsley. Taste and add salt if necessary. Re-heat, stirring to blend well. Spoon into greased shells or ramekins and top with buttered crumbs. Bake in a 350-degree oven for fifteen to twenty minutes or until browned.

QUICK TARTAR SAUCE

This not very sophisticated, but it's still a fine accompaniment for deviled crab.

Mayonnaise
Onion or scallion, (mostly juice) very finely minced
Green pickle relish, well drained
Salad olives, well drained and chopped fine
Worcestershire sauce

We don't give quantities, because this is a natural for ad-lib production. Start with the mayonnaise (about one cup), add the relish, Worcestershire sauce and olives with pimento, deciding as you go along how much of each component will make the sauce right for you. The sauce can be kept in a jar in the refrigerator if not used all at once. It is better made early in the day you plan to use it, so that the flavors get time to blend.

Crab Newburg

A classic seafood dish is Crab Newburg. We wondered for years where it got its name. Seeing it sometimes spelled "Newburgh," we thought that might be an affectation of elegance, or that the dish might be named for the city in New York. Now we've heard a story about the origin.

It seems that in New York City around the end of the last century, a gentleman named Wenburg dined frequently at a restaurant famous for its seafood dishes. He became a friend of the restaurateur who, when he created a new seafood concoction, honored one of his star customers by calling it Crab Wenberg. Later the relationship between the two deteriorated, and the restaurateur changed the first syllable of the name to Newburg and deprived Mr. Wenburg of his place in the index of crab-meat cookery.

In preparing this dish, as well as others that require the addition of beaten egg yolks to the basic béchamel sauce, it is important to remember to beat the eggs with some cold milk, and then gradually to add the hot cream sauce, stirring all the while.

CRAB NEWBURG #1

1 1/2 cups milk (or milk
   and cream)
2 1/2 tbs. butter
3 tbs. flour
1/2 tsp. paprika
1/4 tsp. salt
Dash mace
Dash cayenne
1/2 cup sherry
3 egg yolks, beaten
1 lb. crab meat

Heat one cup of milk to boiling. Melt butter in a very heavy pan, add flour, and mix on a low heat for three or four minutes, until frothy. Stirring with a wire whisk, add hot milk all at once. Continue stirring to insure smoothness. Add paprika, salt, mace, cayenne, and sherry. Mix half a cup of cold milk with the beaten egg yolks in mixing bowl. Slowly add the hot sauce to the egg mixture, stirring with the whisk constantly. Then put the sauce back in the pan. Add the crab meat and stir. Heat slowly and thoroughly. Serve on toast or in patty shells. Serves 4.

CRAB NEWBURG #2

- 4 1/2 tbs. butter or margarine
- 1/2 cup fresh mushrooms, sliced
- 1 lb. crab meat
- 1/2 cup sherry, marsala, or madeira
- 1 1/2 cups milk (or milk and cream)
- 2 cubes chicken stock
- 3 tbs. flour
- 1/4 tsp. mace
- 1/2 tsp. salt
- 2 tbs. brandy
- 3 egg yolks, beaten

In one and one half tablespoons butter, saute mushrooms lightly and set aside. Put crab meat and sherry in a pan and heat slowly. Heat one cup of milk with the chicken cubes. In a heavy pan, melt two and one half tablespoons butter, add flour, and stir for two or three minutes until frothy. Add the hot liquids and stir with a wire whisk; add salt and mace. To crab and sherry, add brandy and set aflame. When flame has died down, add the mushrooms. Now, add one half cup cold milk to beaten eggs, beating with the whisk. Add a bit of the hot sauce, stir well and gradually add the rest of the hot mixture, stirring with the whisk all the while. Put back in the heavy pot. Add the crab and brandy mixture and heat slowly. Serve on toast or in patty shells. Serves 4.

CHARLESTON MEETING STREET CRAB MEAT

Our summer neighbor and fellow crab devotee, Dot Shellender, shares this crab entree with us. It's an interesting transplant from South Carolina to Bucks County, Pennsylvania, where Dot obtained the recipe from the Black Bass Hotel.

4 tbs. butter	4 tbs. sherry
4 tbs. flour	1 lb. crab meat (back fin)
1/2 pint cream	3/4 cup sharp cheddar
Salt and pepper	cheese, grated

Melt butter and blend in flour over low heat. Remove pan from heat. Heat cream and slowly add to butter mixture until smooth. Return to heat and cook slowly until sauce is thickened. Season to taste with salt and pepper. Remove from fire and add sherry and crab meat. Pour mixture into a buttered casserole or individual baking dishes. Sprinkle with grated cheese and bake in a 350-degree oven, uncovered, for twenty to twenty-five minutes. Serves 4.

CRAB CREPES

We first ate crab crepes in a little French restaurant in New York, where they were served rolled up as a first course or extended into a *gateau* as an entree. We were delighted with the idea of wedding crabs to crepe, and tried several variations at home. Now that crepes are in and even the biscuit mix makers have a recipe for making crepes on their packages we recalled the enchanting *gateau*.

We don't give the basic crepe recipe here—those thin pancakes are simple to produce and it should be easy for you to find a recipe. Maybe you even have one of those fancy crepe makers. So, make some crepes and try crab as a new filling. Any of the creamed crab recipes will do nicely—Newburg, Mornay, Last Minute Crab Casserole, etc. Make the sauce thick. Save some of the crab mixture after you have filled the crepes, and thin it down to use over the crepes.

If you want to serve rolled crepes, spoon some crab filling on the crepe and roll it up. Saute lightly in butter or margarine, and spoon on more of the same crab filling, thinned down.

To make a layer cake or *gateau*, here's the procedure. Lightly grease a baking pan. Put one crepe in, then spoon on some crab filling. Put another crepe on top, and again add filling. Use four crepes for each *gateau*, ending with a crepe on top. Ladle sauce over the whole thing.

You can make the crepes and the filling in the morning and make the *gateaux* about one half hour before serving. Warm the sauce and assemble the *gateaux*. Put in a 350-degree oven to heat through. Try sprinkling the tops with a little grated cheese before the oven warming. Use pimento or parsley as a garnish.

Don't be afraid to try variations. If mushrooms are plentiful, add some to the sauce. Or make a vari-layered *gateau* by using the crab mixture for one layer, mushrooms for another. Or make a Florentine mound, using spinach for the bottom layer.

Better yet, invent your own crab-layered crepes.

LEMON-BUTTERED CRAB MEAT

It isn't necessary to be elaborate with crab cookery. If you're tired of sauces and sigh at the thought of getting out herbs and spices and dirtying up all those utensils and pans, try this. It's the closest thing to the crab meat you enjoy when using that primitive approach, hard shell crab feasting. The taste is very close, but your hands won't be soiled. The presentation is elegant enough for wine goblets and linen napkins and its preparation is the essence of simplicity.

1 lb. crab meat (back fin, if possible)	Juice of one lemon, strained
1/2 lb. butter, or margarine	Fresh parsley, chopped
	4 lemon wedges

Heat the oven to 400 degrees. Grease four shells or other ovenproof individual casseroles. Carefully pick over the crab meat and divide it among the shells. Apportion the butter in dots on top of each. Sprinkle with the lemon juice.

Put the shells on a cookie sheet and bake briefly in the hot oven. In about six minutes, they should be golden brown and ready to be topped with the parsley and lemon wedges and served. Serves 4.

Being conscientious energy-savers, of course you will plan to bake some other items, now that you've got a hot oven.

Crab Cakes

Next to hard shell crabs in the newspaper-on-the-table manner, many crab consumers seem to prefer their Chesapeake crustacean converted into crab cakes. Knowing that a tidal wave of protest might swell from Turkey Point to Tangier Island, we still must voice our judgment: crab cakes are usually dull—not abominable, merely uninteresting. As a quick lunch, as a substitute for a hot dog, a crab cake sandwich is welcome, but it's never an adventure in tempting taste.

Our aversion stems, in part, from having eaten so many crab cakes fried in the same deep fat that served too many other items, and we definitely warn against ordering them deep fried if they are available pan-fried. Even so, we've concluded that crab cakes are for those who do not really like crabs. Those folks can always be sure they won't be offended by "too much" of a crab taste when they order crab cakes in a restaurant. They are the same people, probably, who like fish that "doesn't taste like fish." And that's the key to our being underwhelmed by crab cakes—they usually have so much bread crumbs as filler that the succulent crab flavor is subdued, if not buried.

However, crab cakes do not require lump meat; they can be fabricated from claw meat, and they please many people. So, here are a couple of recipes. The shores of the Chesapeake Bay abound with hundreds of variations on this theme.

MARYLAND LADY CRAB CAKES

This is a recipe from a booklet distributed by the state of Maryland. We suspect it is called "lady crab cakes" because it

provides a way of using the meat from female crabs not large enough to compete with the males as steamed hard shell crabs. It uses Italian seasoned bread crumbs instead of plain bread crumbs seasoned to the cook's careful tasting.

1 cup Italian seasoned bread crumbs	1/4 tsp. black pepper
1 large or 2 small eggs	1 tsp. Worcestershire sauce
1/4 cup mayonnaise	1 tsp. dry mustard
1/2 tsp. salt	1 lb. crab meat
	Fat or oil for frying

In a bowl, mix bread crumbs, egg, mayonnaise, and seasonings. Add crab meat and mix gently, but thoroughly. Shape into 6 or 8 cakes. Fry in hot fat (350 degrees) until browned, or pan fry in a little butter, oil or margarine until browned on both sides. (We recommend a mixture of oil and butter, or oil and margarine for pan frying.) Serves 3 or 4.

HARRY BECK'S CRAB CAKES

Our friend, Harry Beck, who is an expert foreign car mechanic, shows with this recipe that he also has some expertise in the kitchen. These crab cakes are pleasantly moist and tasty.

- 1 lb. crab meat
- 2 eggs, beaten
- 1/2 cup fine cracker crumbs
- 3 tbs. mayonnaise
- 2 tbs. onion, finely minced
- 1 tbs. green pepper, finely minced
- 1 tsp. prepared mustard (we use Dijon type)
- Salt and pepper to taste
- Butter and/or oil for pan frying

Mix all the ingredients together. Spoon into iron frying pan in which butter and oil have been heated. Brown only a few minutes on each side. Serves 6.

Soft Shell Crabs

When you're fortunate enough to catch soft shell crabs—or buy them alive—you have to clean them before cooking. The frozen ones come already cleaned. To clean the live soft shell, first cut out the protrusion at the front center of the crab, between the two claws. It's what passes for the head on a crab, and can be cut out with a knife or scissors. Then reach in behind that area and pull out the sack you'll find just inside. Next, lift the tips of the shell, one at a time, and scrape out the "devil's fingers" as you do with steamed hard shells. Finally, pull off the apron at the bottom. The rest of the shell, including the top, is good to eat.

Libby Steinlein, who first introduced us to the Chesapeake and its charms, including crabs, is a native of the Eastern Shore who has spent many years around the bay and has a way with crabs. She cooks soft shells the way we think they are best—sautéed.

LIBBY'S SAUTÉED SOFT SHELLS

1 dozen soft shell crabs
Flour
Salt and pepper

Butter and oil (we use corn oil)
Lemon wedges
Minced parsley

Dry the cleaned soft shells on paper towels. Dredge them with the flour seasoned with salt and pepper. Shake them so that the flour coating is very light. Heat the butter and oil together in a heavy skillet. Saute the soft shells until they are light brown and crisp, turning to get both sides done. Remove to a hot platter, top with minced parsley and serve with lemon wedges.

This will serve 4 or 6 persons, depending on the size of the crabs and the appetite of the diners.

Without doubt, this is the simplest and tastiest way to cook soft shells. They may be fried in deep fat, after being dipped in eggs and crumbs, if you prefer. We think that hides the delicacy of the crab flavor.

Soft shells are delicious cooked under the broiler, but that means having to baste them; heating up the kitchen. So, we always saute them. The taste is very similar.

Crab Imperial

We do not know any emperors, but if one ever happens to show up in our neighborhood on the Chesapeake looking for excellent native food, we'll take him up to Schaefer's Canal House in Chesapeake City, where the Crab Imperial is at its most imperial—indeed, crab nonpareil. The Canal House recipe is a closely-guarded secret, but we have one that's very similar. We found it in a small cookbook called *Mealtime Magic* compiled years ago by the children in the remarkable little elementary school our children attended in the Village of Arden, where we live eight months of the year. In that book, we latched onto Beulah Derrickson's Crab Imperial.

Beulah tells us this is a very old "authentic" Baltimore recipe which she likes because it is simple and does not attempt to "enhance" the crab. Beulah quotes Mrs. Millard Tawes, wife of a former Maryland governor, who firmly believed that "crab cannot be enhanced—only complemented."

You will note that this recipe does not contain green pepper, which is an ingredient in most other Imperial recipes. You may add some, finely minced, if you like. Beulah prefers to omit it, and so do we.

BEULAH'S CRAB IMPERIAL

1 lb. crab meat (back fin)
1 tsp. prepared mustard
1/8 lb. butter
2 1/2 tbs. mayonnaise
1 egg, beaten
Chopped parsley (optional)
Lemon juice (optional)
Buttered bread crumbs

Mix mustard, butter, mayonnaise and egg together and combine with crab meat. Place in casserole. Sprinkle buttered crumbs on top. Bake a half hour at 350 degrees. Serves 3 or 4.

RHODA'S CRAB

We asked our friend and long-time neighbor, Jean Brachman, who is a wizard of a cook, to share a favorite crab recipe with us. She responded with this member of the Crab Imperial family, a recipe supplied her by friend Rhoda, who earns a culinary crown with this entry.

1 lb. back fin crab meat	1/2 tsp. dry mustard
1/2 green pepper, chopped	1/4 tsp. salt
1/2 pimento, chopped	1/4 tsp. white pepper
1 tbs. lemon juice	4 tbs. fine bread crumbs
1 tsp. Worcestershire sauce	2 tbs. butter
1/2 cup mayonnaise	Paprika
3 drops Tabasco	

Set oven at 375 degrees. Combine all but last three ingredients. Rub the butter into the crumbs with your fingers. Set aside. Divide the crab mixture into six or eight shells. Top with buttered bread crumbs. Sprinkle with paprika. Bake fifteen minutes until bubbly. Serves 4.

LAST MINUTE CRAB CASSEROLE

When you have some crab meat in the refrigerator, but get back from the beach too late to be as elaborate about dinner as you had planned, here's a tasty, easy solution to the problem of what to serve 6 people.

1 can condensed cream of mushroom soup
2 cubes chicken stock
1/2 soup can milk
1 tbs. vermouth
1 lb. crab meat
1 pkg. frozen peas, uncooked
Dash cayenne
Salt
1/2 cup Swiss cheese, grated
Paprika

Heat oven to 350 degrees. Rub casserole or shells with margarine. Heat the soup and add the chicken cubes, milk, and vermouth. Add the crab meat, uncooked peas, and cayenne. Taste before adding salt or additional seasoning. Place in the casserole or individual shells and top with grated cheese. Sprinkle paprika over all. Bake about twenty minutes until lightly browned.

CRAB MEAT QUICHE

1 1/2 cups crab meat
1 tbs. celery, finely chopped
1 tbs. scallion, finely chopped
2 tbs. parsley (including stems), finely chopped
3 tbs. sherry
Pastry for 9-inch pie shell or frozen pie shell
4 eggs, beaten
1 cup milk
1 cup light cream
1/4 tsp. mace
1/2 tsp. salt
1/4 tsp. white pepper

Try to make sure the crab meat is free of shell and cartilage. (Go ahead, try!) Put the first four ingredients in the sherry and refrigerate one hour. Heat oven to 450 degrees. Bake the pastry shell for five minutes. Put the crab meat mixture evenly in the pie shell. Combine the rest of the ingredients and add to the pie shell. Bake for fifteen minutes at 450; reduce heat to 350 and bake about ten minutes more (or until a knife inserted one inch from edge of shell comes out clean.) Serve small pieces as hors d'oeuvre or larger slices as a main luncheon course for 6.

OPEN-FACE CRAB MEAT AND CHEESE SANDWICH

This is another treasure from our neighbor Dot's collection. This recipe will serve a gem of a lunch for 6.

- 1 lb. crab meat (back fin preferred)
- Dash Tabasco
- 1 tsp. Worcestershire sauce
- 1 tsp. lemon juice
- 1/4 cup mayonnaise
- 12 slices white bread, toasted
- 12 slices American Cheese
- 5 tbs. tartar sauce
- Paprika

Blend the first five ingredients, after picking over crab meat to remove bits of cartilage and shell. Cut six of the slices of toast in half, diagonally. Spread tartar sauce on all the toast. Place on a cookie sheet, arranged into six servings—one whole slice of toast flanked by two triangles. Spread the crab mixture so that toast is covered; add a slice of cheese to each serving. Sprinkle the tops with paprika and put under broiler until bubbly.

Prepare for the enhancement of your reputation as an inventive cook, as your guests spread reports of this tasty luncheon.

CRAB SALAD

- 2 cups crab meat (back fin preferred)
- 4 tbs. celery (including some tops), finely chopped
- 1 good-sized Winesap apple, finely chopped
- 2 tbs. parsley, minced
- 1 tsp. mustard (Dijon type)
- 1/2 cup (or more) mayonnaise
- 1/2 tsp. Worcestershire sauce
- Salt
- Dash cayenne
- White pepper
- 1/2 tbs. lemon juice
- 2 eggs, hard-cooked and chopped

This mixture handsomely serves 4 to 6 persons, and is a superb cold crab dish. It's astonishing that apple does not appear more often as an ingredient in crab salad recipes.

CRAB STUFFED TOMATOES

Here's an exception to our aversion to the tomato-crab combination. It relies on both the tomatoes and crab meat being sweet and lovely, as both are when freshly picked.

6 large fresh tomatoes
Salt and pepper
3 tbs. butter or margarine
1/4 cup fresh parsley, minced
2 tbs. scallion, minced
1 lb. crab meat
1 tbs. lemon juice
1 tbs. dry vermouth (optional)
1/4 cup grated Swiss cheese
1/4 cup fine bread crumbs

Remove the stem ends and centers with seeds from the tomatoes, and sprinkle with salt and pepper. Melt the butter and add to it the scallion, parsley, crab meat, lemon juice, and vermouth. Mix carefully to blend, but try not to break up the crab meat. Put crab mixture in the tomatoes in a greased shallow baking dish. Sprinkle the tops of the tomatoes with the cheese and crumbs which you have combined. Bake for about twenty minutes in a 350-degree oven. Serves 6.

Crab Goes To The Cocktail Party

When the crab harvest is heavy, we enjoy the luxury of having our favorite seafood to spice the cocktail snacks we serve ourselves and our guests. We whip up a crab dip often, rarely repeating ourselves. To the crab meat, we add mayonnaise, a choice of light seasoning, maybe a bit of finely minced celery, and the result is the hit of the tray.

Another excellent cold treat for cocktail time is crab fingers, described earlier in the section on how to pick crab meat.

CRAB MEAT WITH LEMON

If you have a good supply of back fin crab meat, put a toothpick in each large lump and drop a little lemon juice on each. That's all. You get the unadorned beauty of the crab flavor.

DEVILISH CRAB EGGS

6 eggs, hard-cooked
1/4 tsp. Dijon mustard
1/4 tsp. parsley (used dried, if necessary), finely minced
1/4 tsp. onion salt
1 tsp. curry powder
2 dashes Worcestershire sauce
Dash mace
Salt
1/2 cup crab meat (claw will do)

Halve shelled eggs lengthwise. Set whites aside. Mash yolks thoroughly in bowl. Add all ingredients except salt and crab and mix well. Fold in crab meat and taste. Add salt if needed. Heap mixture into egg whites. Serve chilled.

HOT CRAB MEAT HORS D'OEUVRE

1 cup crab meat
2 tbs. lemon juice
1 cup sour cream
1/4 cup mayonnaise
1 tsp. onion, finely minced
1/4 tsp. chives, finely minced
3 drops Tabasco
1/2 tsp. Worcestershire sauce
1 tsp. garlic salt
Dash white pepper

In a heavy pot, add lemon juice to crab meat and toss. In a separate bowl, mix all the other ingredients, add to the crab, and on a low heat, stir but do not boil. This is good for a chafing dish. Serve with assorted mild crackers.

CRAB PUFFS

1/2 lb. crab meat
2 or 3 scallions, finely minced
1/2 cup cheddar cheese, grated
1 tsp. Worcestershire sauce
1/2 tsp. dry mustard
1 cup water
1/4 lb. margarine or butter
1/4 tsp. salt
1 cup flour
4 eggs

Here's a time when claw meat and shred and bits of other crab meat are as useful as back fin. Mix the first 5 ingredients together. Set aside. Combine the butter, salt, and water in heavy enamelled pot and bring to boiling. Remove and add all the flour, beating until mixture forms a ball. This is hard work. When it leaves side of pan, add the eggs one at a time, beating thoroughly at each addition. Blend in crab mixture and drop by teaspoonfuls onto an ungreased baking sheet. Bake fifteen minutes at 400 degrees; reduce temperature to 350 and bake ten minutes more. Serve hot. This will make more than four dozen appetizers, fit for the most elegant party.

TINY CRAB BALLS

Here's one of the few times we recommend deep fat frying. In this instance, it can produce a very interesting addition to your hors d'oeuvres collection.

1 1/2 tsp. onion, grated
2 tbs. melted butter or margarine
2 tbs. flour
1/2 cup milk
1 scant tbs. vermouth
Yolk of 1 small egg
1/4 tsp. Worcestershire sauce
Dash cayenne
Salt and pepper
1 cup crab meat (body and claw)
1 tbs. parsley, very finely minced
1/2 cup (or less) fine dry bread crumbs.

Saute the onion only until translucent in butter in a heavy pot. Add flour and stir in with wire whisk until foamy. Heat the milk and vermouth and add, stirring constantly with wire whisk. Cook several minutes. Beat the egg yolk with the seasonings; add a little of the hot sauce to the egg, then add this to the sauce in the pot, stirring constantly. It will be very thick. Add the crab and parsley. Stir to blend, then cool. Taste, adding more salt if needed. Shape into very small balls and roll them in the crumbs. Using a basket, fry in corn oil until brown (two to three minutes). Drain well on paper towels. Spear on toothpicks. This will make about 40 crab balls.

CHESAPEAKE CANAPES

1 cup crab meat
1 tsp. Dijon-type mustard
1 tsp. parsley, very finely minced
2 tbs. mayonnaise
Salt and pepper

Dash cayenne
2 tsp. lemon juice
2 tbs. grated Parmesan cheese
1 tbsp. fine bread crumbs
6 slices white bread

Combine the crab meat with the mayonnaise, bread crumbs, and seasonings. Add the salt and pepper to taste. You may not need quite so much lemon juice. Toast the six slices of white bread from which you have removed the crusts. Cut each slice into six squares. Spread them with the crab mixture. Place under the broiler for a few minutes, until brown and bubbly. Saltines can be used, or melba toast.

CRAB SPREAD

Here's an easy crab spread that's very simple to concoct and it's guaranteed to produce appreciative purrs among the hors d'oeuvres nibblers. You may, after tasting it, decide on added taste embellishments. Go ahead, be adventurous!

1 8 oz pkg. cream cheese	1/4 to 1/2 tsp. curry powder
1 cup crab meat (body and claw)	Salt and pepper to taste
	1 tbs. lemon juice (optional)

Mash the cream cheese. Add the crab meat and blend well. Add the curry and mix further. Taste. Add more curry and salt and pepper if you like. Bake in a 400-degree oven for fifteen to twenty minutes. Serve with crackers. (We use a rather shallow, round enamel on iron bake-and-serve container for this, buttering the pan first.)

Try Your Own

Unless you use too much of a spice, or a spice that is too heavy for crab, you will find it easy to try your own variations for crab canapes. Try finely chopped apple and celery, for instance. Tarragon, either fresh or freshly dried, mixed with mayonnaise and lemon makes an interesting diversion. Some people enjoy finely chopped olives and pimento as part of the mix. Who knows? You may happen on a masterpiece.

A NOTE ON NUTRITION

The Virginia Institute of Marine Science is one of our favorite authorities on seafood. A publication of the institute contained the following expert statement on "Seafood Nutrition—Fact and Fancy."

"How many times have you heard that fish is 'brain food?' Or that eating oysters makes you more amorous?

"The idea that eating fish enhances your brain dates back to the nineteenth-century and a Harvard University scientist. He discovered that compounds containing phosphorus are abundant in the brain. So he urged people to eat fish, which is rich in phosphorus. The scientist reasoned that increased amounts of phosphorus in the brain would increase brain power—a concept that has since been disproved.

"Oysters contain cholesterol, the basic building block for both male and female sex hormones. But the body produces enough cholesterol to satisfy our total needs. The additional cholesterol will not affect sexual behavior.

"Seafood won't improve your IQ or act as a love potion. But it is high in protein and low in fat—a combination that makes seafood attractive to dieters. Many people have also learned that seafood is low in sodium and high in potassium. This combination is especially attractive to people with heart problems. Sodium causes the body to retain water and aggravates high blood pressure; potassium tends to negate the effects of sodium.

"Part of developing a nutritional label for seafood involves determining if the nutrients present in fish are also available to the human body. The minerals in a food product may pass through the body instead of being used. For example, fish, which is considered a low moderate source of iron, is not a source of iron in the human body. But fish may help make the iron in other products available to humans. Seafoods may enhance the uptake of iron in foods such as spinach, wheat, and soybeans which have iron normally not available to the human body. Similarly, the protein in fish helps enhance the availability of other minerals to the body.

"The nutrients in seafood work in concert with the body and the other foods we consume. Fish has an important place in the four food groups and provides a good substitute for red meat in the meat group.

"If you eat seafood twice a week, you can cut down on calories and add variety to your eating habits. Variety is the essence of good nutrition, and seafood, in particular, provides a sound complement of protein, minerals, and fats to give you the balance you need."